"I have worked with Kate Wilde for over 15 years, and I can tell you, this woman knows what she's talking about. The most outlandish challenge you've had with your child...she's probably tackled it a hundred times. And that's why I'm so excited that she's written such an incredibly useful book for parents. *Autistic Logistics* is just outstanding! It's a treasure trove of extremely practical techniques to enable your child to triumph over the everyday obstacles that no one else is truly helping you to deal with. And it shows you how to do this in a way that is honoring and respectful of your child. As someone who has worked with thousands of families with children on the spectrum— and overcome autism myself—I can tell you that this book will be a game-changer for you and your family."

—*Raun K. Kaufman, author of* Autism Breakthrough
and Director of Global Education, Autism Treatment Center of America®

"If you, like me, are the parent of a child with autism, *Autistic Logistics* is an absolute must-read. No matter what therapy you're doing with your child, this book will transform your entire home experience. Trying to toilet-train your child? Want to help your child move beyond meltdowns? Looking for your child to get dressed—and stay dressed? The step-by-step instructions in *Autistic Logistics* will help you make it happen—much more quickly than you'd expect! What's more, it will show you how to surmount day-to-day challenges in a way that goes with your child, not against your child. Kate Wilde, who has personally worked with my son, really gets it. She knows all of our challenges, and her fantastic book helps us to overcome them."

—*Kristin Selby Gonzalez, President, Autism Hope Alliance (AHA)*

Autistic
LOGISTICS

A Parent's Guide to Tackling Bedtime,
Toilet Training, Tantrums, Hitting,
and Other Everyday Challenges

Kate C. Wilde

Jessica Kingsley *Publishers*
London and Philadelphia

The Son-Rise Program® is a registered trademark of Barry Neil Kaufman and
Susan Marie Kaufman.
The Autism Treatment Center of America® is a trademark of The Option Institute
and Fellowship.

First published in 2015
by Jessica Kingsley Publishers
73 Collier Street
London N1 9BE, UK
and
400 Market Street, Suite 400
Philadelphia, PA 19106, USA

www.jkp.com

Library of Congress Cataloging in Publication Data
A CIP catalog record for this book is available from the Library of Congress

British Library Cataloguing in Publication Data
A CIP catalogue record for this book is available from the British Library

ISBN 978 1 84905 779 0
eISBN 978 1 78450 016 0

Printed and bound in Great Britain

MIX
Paper from
responsible sources
FSC
www.fsc.org   FSC® C013056

To my mother, Elizabeth Wilde McCormick—thank you for your amazing and continual support, love, and wisdom.

CONTENTS

ACKNOWLEDGEMENTS

I have so many people, wonderful people, to be hugely thankful for. I think of every child that I have worked with and every family who has invited me into their life at times of great despair and joy. These wonderful experiences are in the pages of this book. Thank you for sharing your life with me. To every staff member at the Autism Treatment Center of America, thank you for your dedication, your love, and your excellence in helping children and their families from all over the world. William Hogan, who I co-teach with, thank you for teaching with me every day for the last 20 years! To Raun Kaufman for traveling the world and sharing our amazing work. To Bears and Samahria Kaufman, your love, dedication, and trust in me has helped me grow into the teacher I am today. Thank you for creating this amazing work and offering it to me with such enthusiasm and tenderness. To my sister Nicky, thank you for taking the time to read this book and giving me your support and feedback.

However, there are two people in particular who have poured hours of love and care into this book. My mom, Elizabeth Wilde McCormick, thank you for being my first role model of what it is to be an independent strong woman in the world, and for teaching me the importance of doing "meaningful" work. Thank you so much for your continual support, inspiration, and belief in me. You never gave up on the vision of this book and helped me birth it into the light of day, with your great feedback and wisdom.

To my best friend and Son-Rise Program teacher Bryn Hogan. You spent so many hours reading and editing this book. You went above and beyond to transform this book into a better version of itself. Thank you for your love and wisdom. For your feedback, great clarity, and wonderful attitude. Thank you above all for your amazing friendship.

Heartfelt thanks goes to everyone at Jessica Kingsley, in particular to Lisa Clark. Thank you, Lisa, for standing by my book and for being its champion.

MY STORY

I was 13 when I decided to work with children on the autism spectrum. The catalyst and inspiration for this decision was a movie called *Son-Rise: A Miracle of Love*. I watched this with my twin sister, Nicky. Its funny how the same incident can mean so much to one person and nothing to another. My sister does not even remember watching the movie, but to me it was the beginning of everything. It was my first introduction to autism and I was completely intrigued and fascinated by it. I became the kind of teenager who only read the Cliffs Notes for her school-assigned books because she was too busy reading other books on child development. It was also my first introduction to the concept that love and acceptance is the most powerful force for healing and change. Luckily my 13-year-old brain was still open enough to receive the powerful truth of this message.

The movie *Son-Rise: A Miracle of Love* is the real-life story of Samahria and Barry Neil Kaufman, whose son was diagnosed with severe autism and an under-30 IQ at 18 months, and their journey to help him. In the 1970s there was little available in the way of autism treatments as at that time only 1 in 10,000 children were affected. At that time, harsh behavior-modification techniques, including electric shock, were being used to treat severe autism, and this was not something they wanted for their son. The Kaufmans searched for help for their son and were told repeatedly that autism was a life-long condition and that there was no chance for their son to lead a normal life, or even learn very basic skills to take care of himself. Doctors advised institutionalization. Instead of going with the treatments they were offered by professionals, they decided to work with their son themselves. They took a very different approach from the mainstream thinking and attitudes of that time. Instead of viewing their son's unique behaviors of hand flapping and rocking as a tragic sign of his "terrible disorder," they took a different view.

They decided to see him as a gift in their life. They decided to approach him not with disapproval or fear, but with love and acceptance. Instead of forcing him to conform to their world, they decided to "Join" him in his. They saw his repetitive behaviors as a doorway into his world, so when he flapped his hands, they flapped theirs. When he rocked back and forth, they rocked with him. By Joining him in his world, they were able to make a connection between them. They worked with their son 12 hours a day for three and a half years. Today he shows no signs of his condition and he travels the world lecturing about autism and The Son-Rise Program and is the author of the book *Autism Breakthrough: The Groundbreaking Method That Has Helped Families All Over the World*. Ironically, all these years later, I can say that the little boy that I once saw depicted in that movie when I was 13 years old, the little boy who was the center of a movie that changed my life, is and has been my dear friend for the last 23 years.

Special note: Joining is a technique that is used to help and connect with our children when they are engaging in their repetitive behaviors/stims/isms. Please go to www.autismtreatment.com if you would like to know more about it.

From that point onwards working with children on the autism spectrum became my dream, my focus, and one of the great passions of my life. Throughout my teenage years I would spend my summer holidays and spare time working in play schemes and after-school programs where I might encounter special children, and most importantly children with autism. One summer, to my great delight, I met my first child with autism; I was 15 and she was 14. She wore a helmet because she would bang her head, and was at least a foot taller than me due to the specially designed high-heeled shoes she wore to accommodate her toe walking. I was assigned to her for the day, and within seconds of our meeting she got me in a headlock and started walking, dragging me along. She walked straight out of the school building and headed for the white line in the soccer field. The only knowledge I had about autism and how to be with a child with autism was the movie I had watched. It had left me with two ideas: Join the child in their own world and love and accept what they wanted, which in this case was to walk around the soccer field. So I concentrated as much as I could on enjoying the white line and the walking, and felt good that at least she wanted me with her. She was assigned to me for the rest of the summer, because when she was with me she never banged her head. This was my very first sign of the healing power of Joining. We walked, laughed, played, and had the best time together. She was my first real-life encounter with autism, and I was hooked.

My second encounter was with a child of a family friend. He was three years old when I met him and was such a sweetheart. He loved to run back and forth and back and forth again from one wall to the other and turn light switches on and off. Again when I was with him I focused on Joining him in his activities and loving and enjoying being with him. I noticed how he would look at me and smile when I ran with him and was touched by the loveliness of his personality. Seeing glimpses of his personality shine forth as I Joined him consolidated the idea that there was a complete person inside this silent boy, and I wanted to find a way to reach him and help him communicate to the world. This only solidified my belief that Joining a child in their activities was an incredible way to connect with them.

I went on to college to study music and education at Surrey University. I chose music because it was a subject I was good at and I had the idea that I might become a music therapist. The more I learned about music therapy the more I realized it was not the therapy for me. I think it is a wonderful therapy that does great work with children with autism, but for me it was too restricted; I wanted to work in a more varied way. I was still itching to work directly one on one with children with autism in a therapeutic way, and was discouraged with how long it would take until I was allowed to do that. I was told that in order to work directly with children one on one I would have to do more educational work and I did not want to wait—I wanted to work straight away.

Upon leaving university, instead of going for further academic studies, I went to work for Dr. Rachel Pinney, the author of *Bobby: Breakthrough of an Autistic Child* and *Creative Listening* and the founder of Children's Hours in North London. She worked with a variety of children, some who were emotionally disturbed, and a number of children with autism. She truly was a genius with children; they loved her, and she had an incredible ability to connect deeply with them. Like most geniuses she had a colorful character and loved to push people's buttons. She was 80 when I met her, and my initial interview took place while she was taking a bath. After having asked me a few questions about myself, she let me know that I had passed the test. "What test?" I asked. She then informed me that she liked to see how people reacted to different situations. The fact that I was not fazed by her being in the bath led her to believe that I would not be judgmental toward the children I would be working with.

Although she was 80 and walked with the help of crutches, she had a lively mind and soul. As part of my training with her I would accompany her on the different lectures she gave in her surrounding community. I would carry suitcases of books around for her. Amazingly, she carried around the book *Son-Rise* by Barry Neil Kaufman, which was the very story I had watched on television when I was 13! She trained me herself to work one on one with the children, and I spent every day working directly with children with autism. I was in heaven. I was struck by the intelligence and love each child showed me on a daily basis. It was here that I met a family who were going to the United States to participate in a special program for their daughter with autism. Although I had no idea what the program was, I jumped at the opportunity to have this adventure and learn another form of treatment for autism.

It was not until on the second day of the program in America, when they showed us the NBC movie *Son-Rise: A Miracle of Love*, that I realized that this center was run by the family I had watched in the movie, that had inspired me to work with children with autism in the first place. Wow! That was a very awe-inspiring moment for me. I had come full circle, and it was as if in some way I had come home. I knew that I had found the methodology that I wanted to train and work in. Until that point I had never encountered two particular traits found within this methodology. First, the staff were so sincere in their love and delight of the little girl I had come with that you could see it and feel it in everything they did. Second, they were also so powerful and effective in asking her to change and grow. They asked her to look at them, to use the spoken word, to dress herself. They helped her to grow so much during that week, and all within the context of truly enjoying and loving her.

I carried on my work with Dr. Rachel Pinney and then, instead of pursuing further study, I returned to the Autism Treatment Center of America to begin my formal Son-Rise Program training. I trained intensively for five years to become a Son-Rise Program Child

Facilitator and Son-Rise Program Teacher. This is about the same amount of time and energy it would take to get a PhD. My training was extremely hands-on. It is an in-depth training and has a strong emphasis on attitude. I worked directly with children and adults on the autism spectrum and got direct feedback from the senior staff. We were video-taped and then our time with each child analyzed, sometimes frame-by-frame or second-by-second. I also worked directly with parents and other family members, training them on how to work with their children, and received feedback on this. If we were to teach a principle or technique, we would be observed and then our explanations and sharing would be reviewed in detail by our trainers in order to help us to be the most effective communicators possible. We spent hundreds of hours exploring our own thoughts and feelings so that we could truly approach each child and each adult with an open, caring, and accepting heart.

One thing the Son-Rise Program recognizes is that each child with autism can be so different, motivated by different things, and have varying degrees of complex challenges. I needed to be able to recognize these challenges, to connect with and help these children and families from the very start of meeting them. Then I had to be able to articulate what I knew and teach it to many families so that they could work in this way with their own children. This took a lot of time and focus on my part and experience of different children and families to acquire it.

I have now worked with the Son-Rise Program for over 20 years, and feel so blessed to have supported so many children and their families. I have spent thousands and thousands of hours working one on one with the most lovely, silly, funny, determined, and hard-working children and adults. I have never worked with a child who did not want to learn, who did not try their very best. I feel so grateful to have had so much time with each and every one of these children, for they have taught me what it means to open my heart, to listen, and have the daring to try even the things that seem impossible at first. I have been hit, punched, kicked, bitten, spat on, defecated on, peed on, loved, kissed, and danced with, been talked to for hours on end about numerous different subjects from the magnificence of washing machines to the statistics of earthquakes, and I have Joined thousands of unique and wonderful different "isms" ("isms" are what we in the Son-Rise Program call a child's repetitive behavior or "stims").

Although I can never say that I have stopped learning, and am sure that I will encounter many more wonderfully different situations, I can say that I have experienced many that you encounter today with your children. Although your child is unique, I am sure that I have worked with a child who has displayed some of the same behaviors, motivations, nature, or challenges as yours. One of the great parts of my education and training is the depth and breadth of hands-on experience that I have to share with you. I know of no other training that exceeds this. I feel that I can say with confidence from my own heart that although I have never met your child or children, I know that I would love them. Their uniqueness and loveliness would not be lost on me no matter what their behaviors are.

I am now the Director of the Son-Rise Program and I train the staff at the Autism Treatment Center of America to become Son-Rise Program Child Facilitators and Son-Rise Program Teachers. I also teach parents, both individually and in groups, to run the Son-Rise Program with their children. I do this either via the telephone, going to their houses or when they come here to our center. We have parents come to our center from all over the world. I have worked with families from Thailand, Singapore, Africa, Malaysia, China, France, Poland, Russia, Slovakia, Argentina, and Brazil, to name a few, and frequently travel with our staff to Europe to present the Son-Rise Program. It has been such a wonderful journey and I feel so blessed to have met and worked with so many amazing families and their children.

This is why I have written this book. I want to help you and offer you the tools and strategies that will help you build a wonderful life with your very special child and family.

Kate

HOW TO READ THIS BOOK

Everything that I do and say in this book is based on the Son-Rise Program principles and techniques. This book can be used by any parent, therapist, teacher, or family member who loves a child with autism. This book can be used if your primary therapy for your child is ABA, Floortime, RDI, verbal behavior, Handel, intensive play therapy, or any other. This book is truly for anyone and everyone who wants help with the following:

- tooth brushing

- hair cutting

- dressing

- sleeping challenges

- hitting

- tantrums

- toilet training

- introducing new foods.

Most of these things happen outside of set therapy time. These things happen every day, every week, and every month, and this book is designed to help with these and other everyday challenges.

There are many books on the market that talk about these subjects for the typical child, but not for the child on the autism spectrum. You may feel that you are at a loss on how to be with your child outside therapy or school hours; on how to create a harmonious home experience for you, your child, and your family. I hope this book helps you live in harmony with your child and create routines that work for you and your family. This I know can be done.

First, a note about the use of personal pronouns in the book. I have alternated between male and female by chapter and in Exercise 4.1 referring to 'your child' or 'the autistic child' to avoid the frequent clumsy use of *he or she*, etc.

Certain names and identifying characteristics have been changed to protect the privacy of individuals in the stories of this book.

The first six chapters of this book are perspectives and concepts about how to think about and approach your very different child. These chapters will give you a different way to think about your child, or may help solidify what you already know. Either way I encourage you to read these chapters first, as I refer to them in the other chapters. They will help you understand and put into practice the strategies outlined in the other chapters. The whole book will make more sense to you if you do.

The next six chapters are dedicated to specific subjects such as how to deal with your child's tantrums and their hitting, pinching, and biting, toilet training, sleeping, self-help skills, and introducing new foods.

This book is as much about helping you change the way you think about and respond to your child as it is about helping them acquire new skills. I believe that you are the most useful and most loving person your child has in their life. There is nobody who loves or is more dedicated to your child than you. That does not mean that you always know what to do. Many parents feel that they "should" know, but we all know that our children are very different and they did not come with a manual. I know that I had to learn all the things in this book myself. It was not something I was born with. There is no manual on how to respond to your child when they do something that is so different from what you were expecting. I hope that this book will be some sort of a guide for you as you navigate parenting your child.

The beginning of each chapter first explores how we are responding to, and what we are thinking about, what our children do. This is a critical part of the process to help your child acquire the skill you are working on. There will also be exercises included in this section to aid you in this process. Then each chapter outlines many step-by-step practical strategies that you can implement immediately. Also for your convenience there is a checklist at the end of most of the chapters of action items, so you have them all in one place.

If your child does not get the skill you were hoping for this week there is always next week and the week after. Our children are not on the same timeline that we are—sometimes they might require a little more time to understand. The great thing about that is that time is something you can give them. Most people will try things just for a day and then declare that they don't work. I know I have done that with the many diets I have tried over the years. But we all know that we have to stick to the diet over time to see results. Try these suggestions every day for a least a month before you even think of giving up on them. You would not plant a seed and then after seeing no growth for just three days throw it out! You know it takes time for the seed to push down roots and show growth above ground, days of persistent and consistent watering and sun. These strategies are no different; give them the time you would a growing plant.

I know these strategies work because I have implemented them myself and seen them work. I have taught countless parents to implement these strategies and seen them work. These are not theories—they are well-tested practices that the Son-Rise Program has been teaching for over 30 years.

Special note: If you want to read a "how to" book that will explain how to use the Son-Rise Program with your child, you can read *Autism Breakthrough: The Groundbreaking Method That Has Helped Families All Over the World* by Raun K. Kaufman.

Chapter 1

UNDERSTANDING OUR CHILDREN'S EXPERIENCE

This is the most important chapter of the whole book. It will give you the foundation and concepts that will make all the suggestions and strategies in this book be the most effective they can be. It will set the scene for how to approach and teach your very different child.

The first place to start in helping our children is to gain an understanding of their experience. That their sensory processing system behaves differently than ours. It is challenging for them to process sensory input from the world. Their hearing, sense of smell, touch, and vision can be radically different from ours. So much so that just being in the world can be extremely overwhelming, unpredictable, and chaotic.

Let's just take their hearing. They may hear things so much louder than we do, or may hear sounds broken up, like a bad cell phone connection. Some children have difficulty filtering out all the different sounds in their environment, making it near impossible to focus on just one. Think about all the sounds at the mall. You have the background music, people talking, the sounds of the air conditioning, the wheels of all the prams and buggies, the noises from the cash registers, and I could go on and on. What if you could not filter any of these sounds? That you heard them at the same volume tumbling toward you? Would you not want to retreat from that overloaded experience, to cover your ears and find a way to tune it all out? It would be overwhelming for anyone, and that's just our children's audio experience. You can see why our children have a hard time responding to us.

Now let's take a moment and think about our children's sense of smell. This can be amplified for our children, making what is a mild and everyday smell for us unbearable for them. I have seen children shut down completely as a way to block out an overpowering smell. Think of all the different fragrances there are in the world, so many for our sensitive children to navigate. I know for myself that I can get a headache just walking through the cosmetic section of a department store, because of the strong smells of perfume.

Then there is the sense of touch. Some of you may have children who take off all their clothes as soon as they get home from school. Or your child may only wear one particular outfit. For some of our children clothes may feel like sandpaper on their skin. Maybe the closest you can get to knowing what it is like is when you have a very high fever, of how your skin feels like it is burning and is sensitive to other people's touch or even you touching it.

You may notice that your child shows no signs of pain. Or plays outside in the cold snow and shows no signs of being cold. Being less sensitive, it is clear that your child's sensory system is processing touch and sensation very differently.

Let's talk about vision. I have worked with children who only see out of their peripheral vision, meaning they only see what is to the side of them but not what is right in front of them. Others have trouble with their depth perception. Raun K. Kaufman recalls times as a child that he would sometimes see as if he was looking through the wrong end of a pair of binoculars.

Now imagine what it must be like for our children on a daily basis navigating the everyday sounds, sights, smells, and physical touch of our world. Think of a place that is overwhelming for you, maybe it is the mall, airport, or a big concert or festival, or maybe a noisy nightclub. Now imagine on top of that someone asking you to do something that is challenging for you. Wow! No wonder our children want to retreat from the world and create their own ordered world that they can control.

I met Martin, a sweet 12-year-old boy diagnosed with pervasive developmental disorder (PDD) whose parents started consulting with me because the school he was at wanted to expel him. At lunchtime Martin would start to hit other children and try to throw their lunch boxes out the window. He would also resist going into the lunchroom and often tried to run away. His teachers did not know how to handle him anymore. His parents were at their wits' end. His parents and I did Son-Rise Program consultations together, and, instead of thinking that he was just being naughty, we took the approach that he was taking care of himself and we tried to understand how this behavior was helping him. This helped us become true detectives in trying to understand what was going on for him. In the end we found out that he had an over-sensitivity to the smell of bananas; we found this out because bananas were at every one of his outbursts. Martin was unable to communicate that it was the smell that was bothering him, not because he could not talk but because he did not have the knowledge himself that the smell was the challenge. It took a lot of "detective work" to figure this out. Once we knew this, we were able to help him know what to do when he had an "overwhelming" smell, without hitting and running away.

Joe, a very intelligent and funny seven-year-old boy with autism, would hyperventilate when he had to walk across a threshold. It would take him many false starts before he actually made it through, whether it was into a lift or a shop. His mom and dad would get very frustrated as it took them so long to do anything when they were out. They experienced their son as being controlling and difficult, understandably as they did not know why. During consultations together we took the approach that he was doing this for a reason and began to look at what could be happening for him. We discovered that he had no depth perception. Thus being in unfamiliar places was extremely challenging for him. Again, once we knew this was the cause of his many false starts, we could begin to help Joe with the root cause of what was actually happening for him.

These two examples show how differently our children experience the world. It also shows us that although we may not always see the reason, there is always a reason behind why our children do what they do. If we come from this perspective then we can become what in the Son-Rise Program we call "being like a detective" and investigate what the reason could be. This way we actually get to the core reason as to why our children are behaving the way they are, and thus get to help them much more successfully than just trying to change their behavior.

In each of the chapters on the varying subjects I am going to ask you to first become a detective about your child's experience. To try and find out what our children's behavior is trying to solve or achieve. If we take the perspective that they have a reason for what they are doing, like Martin and Joe had, we can then try to find out the reason.

Once we have that information it will be easier to know what to do to help our children acquire the new skills.

So we can already see that our children may experience the world as chaotic, unpredictable, and uncontrollable. Now let's put people into that equation. That's you and me. Although we have the very best of intentions and are doing the best we can, our children often experience us as very unpredictable. People are highly unpredictable and uncontrollable. We move at different speeds—sometimes fast, sometimes slow. We randomly pick our children up and put them in the bath. Take off and put clothes on them. Sometimes we shout, sometimes we sing. Sometimes we are angry, sometimes we are happy. Sometimes we let our children play with their toys, and sometimes we don't. For our children there is no discernible pattern as to when or why we do or do not do these things. For children who may have an over-sensitivity to sound, touch, or visual stimulation, the unpredictable behavior of people is often something that they have to move away from and defend themselves from. Have you ever done one of the following?

- Taken away your child's favorite "stim/ism" toy, hoping that if it is not there he will stop playing with it and interact instead?

- Taken away your child's favorite toy and used it so that he will eat his lunch to get it back?

- Forced the first bit of food into your child's mouth, in the hope that he will see that it is really yummy and will want to eat more?

- Held down your child to brush their teeth so that he will not get a cavity?

- Forced clothes on your child so that he could make it to the school bus?

- Hugged and kissed your child even though he was trying to get out of your embrace?

All of us have probably done one of the above things, because we love our children and we want to find a way to help them. However, when we do this the opposite of what we want happens. Our children get more controlling and less open to what we are suggesting. Why?

Because when we feel forced or pushed, we push back. If someone takes away our favorite toy we will probably think twice before we play with that person again. If someone forced a sweater or coat on us, is it not our first instinct to take it off?

It is interesting that most of our children choose repetitive behaviors (stims/isms) that include objects or parts of their own bodies or speech that they are in control of. If you think about it, it makes total sense. While people are mostly unpredictable and uncontrollable, objects are completely the opposite. They are predictable and controllable. When our children pick up a toy train it always looks the same; it is the same color and has the same smell and feel; when they put it down it stays in the place they put it. It never tries to pick them up or tickle them, it does not take things away from them, and it always does what they want it to do. It is not surprising that our children move away from people and begin to create a world for themselves that mainly consists of interactions with objects, predictable patterns, and the seeking of self-soothing repetitious activities (stims/isms).

The way we change this dynamic and help our children move toward us is to give our children control. We do that by becoming as predictable and as controllable as the objects they love. This book is about the long game—wanting our children to want to eat new foods and wear clothes, or brush their teeth, to actually enjoy these activities without us forcing them.

When we force or try to control our children we teach them that we cannot be trusted. That at any moment we might take away the thing they cherish the most. Or we may hold them down against their will for reasons they do not understand, giving them more reasons to move away from us, and not listen to us. When we force or try to control our children they become more controlling, not less. Instead I suggest you focus your attention in all your actions with your children on "giving them control"—creating instead a rock-solid trust with your children. This trust is essential and the foundation upon which we can encourage them to do the things that are difficult for them. Like sit on the potty. Eat new foods. Get dressed in unfamiliar clothes and brush their teeth. Trust is the most important factor when teaching someone.

Some of our children who have been held down on a regular basis to have their teeth cleaned or their hair cut may have a reflex of starting to cry, or of running away from the mention of a toothbrush or the sight of a pair of hair-cutting scissors. Not because they are afraid of the scissors or hate getting their teeth brushed, but because they have associated these actions/objects with being held down. It is that which they are protesting against. Once we stop doing this, by letting our children know that we will give them control over the situation, we can begin to help our child make friends with the sight of the toothbrush or the hair-cutting scissors, or with exploring a new food. Once we have helped our child make friends with these activities, then and only then can we start the adventure of helping them acquire the new skill. We can give them this control by using the Son-Rise Program Control Protocol outlined below.

USE THE SON-RISE PROGRAM CONTROL PROTOCOL

The Control Protocol is designed to ensure that we always give our children the control they need and never use force. We don't want to get the activity over and done. We want to inspire our children to want to brush their own teeth, to love getting their hair cut and trying new foods. The best way to get there that also leaves your relationship with your child intact is to create ourselves to be as controllable as possible. If we use this protocol in all our interactions with our children we will be giving our children the control they need. In turn you will find that they will become more flexible and less controlling. It has three simple steps.

Step 1—Position yourself in front of your child.

Step 2—Give an explanation.

Step 3—Look for permission.

I will show you how this works in the example of putting a jacket on your child.

Step 1—You would position yourself in front of your child with their jacket. This is so they can clearly see that you are about to do.

Step 2—As you are in front of your child tell them verbally that you are about to put their jacket on. You might say something like: *Holly, we are going to go outside, so I am going to put your jacket on.* It is important that you explain what you want to do before actually trying to do it.

Step 3—(This step is very important.) After you have explained what you are going to do, you wait for permission. This means you look for any indications from your child of "Yes" (it is ok for me for you to put on my jacket) or "No" (I do not want you to put on my jacket). Moving slowly toward them with the jacket, look for a sign that you have permission to put it on them. If your child is verbal they may say yes or no; if they say no, then it is time to give control, by respecting their "No." You may say to them something like this: *Thank you so much for letting me know you do not want the jacket on right now; let's try again in two minutes.* You would then wait two minutes before you try again. If they say yes then you know you have permission so go ahead and put the jacket on.

If your child cannot talk yet, you are going to look for physical cues (do this even if your child can talk, as they may choose not to verbally answer you at this time); notice if they are moving away from you, toward you, or do not move at all as you move toward them. If they move away from you, I would take that as a possible "No" and say something like this: *I see that you are moving away. I'll take that as a no, you do not want me to do this; I'll try again in two minutes.* If your child moves toward you, take that as a yes and say something like: *You are moving toward me; I will take this as a yes. Thanks for letting me know; I like to know what you want.*

If you get no clear response, no indications of "Yes" or "No," take that as an opportunity to try and be a "happy detective." Proceed slowly and explain again what you are doing. Then say: *As you have not moved away from me I am going to try to put your jacket on; if you do not want this just let me know by moving away.*

As you put the jacket on, be vigilant in noticing any physical signs that could indicate that they do not want you to do this. If they move away, stop.

Doing the above protocol sends a number of really helpful and clear messages to your child:

- I will have a chance to say "Yes" or "No."

- My mom listens to me, so it is worth communicating to her.

- I can relax around my mom because she is predictable.

- It is safe to be around my mom.

- Maybe I could try to do what my mom is asking of me because she will let me stop later if I want to.

Remember, using this Control Protocol with your children is the most important ingredient in making every strategy in this book effective.

"No" means… "No"

Another important way to give control to your child is to respect their "No." Not just 50 percent of the time but 100 percent of the time. If you think about it, you don't like it if your "Nos" are not respected. You gravitate towards and choose friends who will respect your "No." You move away from people who don't. It's that simple. The more we respect our child's "No" the more likely they will want to spend time with us and do the things we are asking of them. Trust is everything. If I trust that when I say no to the person I am with they will stop, then I may allow myself to do something that is challenging for me *because* I know I can stop at any time. If I do not trust that with a person there is no way I will do something challenging with them.

Dan, a lovely five-year-old boy with autism, came to our Son-Rise Program Intensive. His parents were extremely worried about how the week would go, because he was extremely reluctant to spend any time with any person who was not his parents and grandmother. They felt that they could not leave him with anyone else or take him to any school situation. I was the first child facilitator to work with him in our specially designed Son-Rise Program playroom that has an en-suite bathroom attached. When he realized that he was alone in the playroom with me he promptly started to cry and pushed me into the bathroom and closed the door, saying very loudly and clearly, "No." From behind the bathroom door I began to talk to him and told him my name, who I was, why I was here, where his parents were and when they would be back, and that I would love to come in and play with him, but that it was up to him. I would be happy to stay in the bathroom for as long as he wanted me to. To which I heard him say a loud and clear "Good." I let around five minutes go by before I told him that I was going to open the bathroom door, to which he said, "No." I celebrated him for telling me this and did not open the door. I did this a few more times, respecting his "No" each time he said it. It took me one hour and 45 minutes of being in the bathroom before he allowed me to open the door. Once I got the door open I still stayed in the bathroom, showing him that I could be trusted and that I was not going to make him do anything he did not want to. After 15 minutes of having the bathroom door open, I told him I was just going to move to the threshold of the door, to which he did not say anything; I took that as a chance to try, and moved to the threshold. Five minutes later I took my first step into the playroom successfully! Once in the playroom I kept my distance and Joined in with what he was doing. That day it took me two hours to get into the same room as him. Later that afternoon it took me only 45 minutes; the next day I could walk immediately into the room and start playing with him, and he never ordered me out again. I know if I had not taken this time initially and given him control he would not have allowed me in later.

"No" only means "No, not now," it doesn't mean "Never."

When our children indicate "No," we stop. Each time they say no, we stop. However, we always ask again. Wait a few minutes, at least *two to five minutes*, and then ask again. If they say no again, then ask again. If after four or five times of asking them every two minutes they turn you down each time, wait at least 15 minutes before asking again. We can give control and be persistent in going for what we want. That's the secret! Give control mixed with persistence.

Take the time in the beginning, it will reap you many, many rewards later. "No" means "No."

EXERCISE 1.1

Take a moment right now and time what two minutes feels like—it is actually a really long time. If you ask again in 20 seconds, which can also feel like a long time, it may feel too pushy for your child and that you are not really listening to their no; two minutes is a nice length of time to show them that you heard and respect their no.

REMOVE CONTROL BATTLES IN YOUR HOUSE

A control battle simply means a time where we have to stop, say no, or take something away from our child. As a way to give our children more control we want to remove any situations where control battles occur. For example, if your child keeps playing with your DVD collection and you keep having to take them away from him, then put the DVDs somewhere where he does not have access to them. Thus you can eliminate one "No" (now only 500 more "Nos" left!). Removing as many "Nos" as we can from our relationship with our child is a way to build trust and is a way to decrease the "fights" we have with our children.

The exercise below will take you through three of the main rooms in your house to highlight any control battles. Use this exercise for each room in your house.

EXERCISE 1.2
SITUATIONS
The kitchen

Go into your kitchen, sit down at your kitchen table or breakfast bar, and think about what happens between you and your child in this room. What does your child do in this room that you do not want them to do? There is a list below that is designed to help you start thinking of different situations. Tick the ones that happen between you and your child, and add others that I may not have mentioned to the list.

- ❐ My child keeps going into the fridge and throwing eggs onto the floor.

- ❐ My child keeps going into the kitchen cabinets and the fridge and eating and drinking food I do not want him to have.

- ❐ My child likes cutlery and will take the cutlery out of the drawers and line them up on the kitchen floor.

- ❐ My child does not understand that the oven is hot and will open and close it even when I am cooking.

- ❐ My child keeps pressing the buttons on the microwave and watches the neon numbers go up and down.

_____

_____

_____

The sitting room

☐ My child will repeatedly turn all the lights off and on.

☐ My child will want me to turn the TV on all the time.

☐ My child will take all the dirt out of the potted plants and either eat it or scatter it on the carpet.

☐ My child will rip all the pages in the books and magazines that are on the shelves or lying around the room.

_____

_____

_____

The bathrooms

☐ My child will empty out all the shampoo bottles.

☐ My child will turn on all the taps and flood the bathroom.

☐ My child will throw things down the toilet.

_____

_____

_____

You can avoid these situations by changing your environment. When thinking about your particular control battles with your child consider these three solutions:

- Move the object.

- Lock or gate the door or cabinet.

- Change access to water.

For example, below are solutions for the areas I mentioned above.

SOLUTIONS
···

The kitchen

- My child keeps going into the fridge and throwing eggs onto the floor. _Solution:_ Get a sturdy lock and put it on your fridge, so that your child has no access to it anymore.

- My child keeps going into the kitchen cabinets and the fridge and eating and drinking food I do not want him to have. *Solution:* Lock the kitchen cabinets, or put a gate at the kitchen entrance so he cannot go into the kitchen when you are not there. Alternatively you could move the food you do not want him to eat to another fridge you keep in your garage or basement that he does not have access to.

- My child keeps pressing the buttons on the microwave and watches the neon numbers go up and down. *Solution:* Move the microwave to a place where your child cannot reach its controls.

The sitting room

- My child will repeatedly turn all the lights off and on. *Solution:* You can get boxes to put over the light switches; you can get these from any hardware store. Or you could move all the light switches so that they are too high for your child to reach.

- My child will want me to turn the TV on all the time. *Solution:* Get rid of your TV! Or you could have one room in your house that has your TV, computer, and other precious things in it, that you keep locked and none of your children are allowed in it. This has worked very well for a number of families I work with. Their children accepted this concept very quickly.

- My child will take all the dirt out of the potted plants and either eat it or scatter it on the carpet. *Solution:* Put the plants up high so he cannot reach them. Or decide to have a plant-free house for a while. This is not forever, just for now, so that you can give more control to your child. You can always introduce plants back into the house later, maybe at a time when they won't be irresistible for your child.

- My child will rip all the pages in the books and magazines that are on the shelves or lying around the room. *Solution:* Put them somewhere where your child will not be able to reach them.

The bathrooms

- My child will empty out all the shampoo bottles. *Solution:* Put them in a locked cabinet. Out of sight, out of mind.

- My child will turn on all the taps and flood the bathroom. *Solution:* Either keep the bathrooms locked, or have a plumber come in and create a switch where you can turn off the water at each sink. This is a great thing to do and will give you peace of mind that your child will not be flooding the house.

- My child will throw things down the toilet. *Solution:* Get a lock for your toilet seat. Yes, there are locks even for toilet seats!

•••••••••••••

Doing this exercise will make your life so much easier! You won't be spending as much time managing your child. You will have the peace of mind that your child can no longer get up to the mischief they used to do. You can become the "Yes" Mom and Dad that you want to be. Not only is that great for you but it also gives our children the sense of control that they crave. And you will have more time to focus on playing and helping your child learn the skills you want them to learn. It's a win-win all round.

USEFUL THOUGHTS THAT WILL SUPPORT YOU IN GIVING CONTROL TO YOUR CHILD

- **Giving control is the technique/goal.** When you are respecting your child's "No" and giving them control, tell yourself that this is a success. This is your objective and a very important part of working with your child and helping them gain independent skills.

- **Believe that giving your child control is more important than the skill itself.** If our children trust us, then they will keep coming toward us to interact with us. If my child says no and I respect this, then I keep the door open for my child to keep coming toward me; thus I am creating many more opportunities for my child to learn this skill in the future. If I give in to my desire to just get things done quickly or take a shortcut and go against my child, then I run the risk of closing the door to future opportunities of my child being open to learning from me.

- **Believe that giving our children control may take longer in the short term, but is shorter in the long term.**

- **Read this chapter more than once.** I would recommend that you reread it each Sunday night, as you start a fresh week parenting your child.

CONTROL ACTION CHECKLIST

- ☐ Think this: My child is not behaving this way to be difficult—there is always reason behind their actions.

- ☐ Become "like a detective" to find the reason behind what your child is doing.

- ☐ Take the fight out of the equation, by not forcing your child into an activity/skill.

- ☐ Think this: *The more control I give my child over their physical body the more flexible and open they will become to doing what I want them to do.*

- ☐ Think this: *We want our child to want to brush their hair or sit on toilet, rather than just getting it over and done with.*

- ☐ Use the three-step Control Protocol every time you physically engage with your child:

  - ☐ Position yourself in front of your child.

  - ☐ Give them an explanation.

  - ☐ Look for permission.

- ☐ Respect your child's indication of "No" 100 percent of the time.

- ☐ If your child says "No," stop. Then try again two to five minutes later.

❐ Remove control battles from each room in your house:

    ❐ Move the object.

    ❐ Stop access to the area.

    ❐ Change access to water.

I am really excited for you to take on and embrace the idea of giving our very different children the control they are looking for. It is my experience that this helps our children enormously—it helps them begin to relax, explore, and move closer to the world of people.

Chapter 2

CREATING CLEAR AND STRONG BOUNDARIES

Creating clear, strong boundaries for our children is the partner to giving them as much control as possible. This may seem confusing, but this combination creates a very safe and well-defined environment, for our special children, their siblings, and for you. Even when we give our children as much control as possible that does not mean that they get everything they want or do everything they want exactly when they want it. You are still the grown-up who is in charge of your household, not the other way around. I know that for some of us reading this book our children may have already taken over the household and we may feel held captive to their demands and wishes 24/7. Believe me, there is help for those of us who feel this way! This chapter will help you regain your leadership of the household by helping you create and implement some clear, loving, and useful boundaries for your children.

I am defining the word "boundary" as a limit we create for our children that helps them both navigate and interact with their environment, and supports their overall health and wellbeing. For instance, one limit could be *Please do not jump with food in your mouth as you could choke.* Another is *You must be in your bed after 7pm.* A boundary is something that stays the same and is consistently held.

Having wanted to work with special children since I was a teenager, I have gone through many different understandings of what I thought would be important for them. In my late teens I believed that they did not really need boundaries or rules, but would organically choose the right thing for themselves. I even remember being enamored with the idea that if you put out a bunch of different foods a child will automatically eat what is balanced and good for them. As my experience grew I realized that children do not always see the bigger picture concerning their overall health, favoring short-term satisfaction over long-term goals. They may choose the chocolate because of its taste, not its nutritional content. They may want to stay up all night playing video games, causing them to sleep through all the beneficial therapies during the daytime. I now see how carefully considered boundaries and rules are important for a child's mental health and add to their comfort and happiness. A child who has enough sleep is often less cranky and can benefit more from their schooling and therapies. A child who has a balanced diet will most likely have fewer health challenges. Creating boundaries and sticking to them is also important for a parent's mental health, empowering them to take charge and create the family life that they feel comfortable with.

Our everyday adult life is edged with boundaries. We must wear a seat belt; we can only drive at or under a certain speed limit; we are not allowed to take things from shops without paying for them first; we are not allowed to hit or kill anyone; and we cannot enter another person's house unless they invite us to, or open another person's mail. If we do any of these actions, we do it knowing that if caught there will be a consequence to our actions.

Imagine what it would feel like if we did not know what we could or could not do. We might be driving along at a nice speed of 30 miles an hour one day and not be given a speeding ticket, then the next day do the same and get given a $100 ticket. If the laws kept changing then we would not feel safe and secure that our actions would not land us in jail or debt. We would not know how to take care of ourselves.

This is how it is for a child whether they are neuro-typical or on the autism spectrum. They want to know what they can and cannot do in their environment, because they want to understand how the world around them works and that it works in some consistent way. It also helps them feel that they are being "looked after"; that their parents are taking care of them, keeping them safe, and will not let them do something that would hurt them. I remember my niece glowering at me after burning herself on a hot pan, and saying crossly: "Why did you let me do that?" She had trusted that I would let her know what was not safe for her. When we feel safe and know what to expect we will explore more, we will learn more, and dare to do things that are challenging for us.

When we give instructions such as *Don't play with matches or knives* or *Don't jump while eating,* we are offering boundaries designed to help a child begin to understand how to take care of their own bodies. These boundaries are an important educational tool for our children. Wherever our children are on the autism spectrum they can understand and learn these boundaries. It is up to us to set them, and teach them as lovingly as we can.

LIMIT YOUR BOUNDARIES TO AS FEW AS POSSIBLE

Keep in mind that giving control is the key to creating a strong relationship with our children. The stronger our relationship is, the more likely they will connect with us, and the more opportunities we will have to teach the life skills discussed in this book. We will want to pick the boundaries for our children very carefully, creating as few as possible. It is important to look at your house and get rid of as many areas of potential "control battles" as possible (see Chapter 1), creating fewer boundaries to enforce.

When we are setting such boundaries it is the only time that we suggest that you do not use the Son-Rise Program Control Protocol. This means that if you are setting a boundary where you are not letting your child play with kitchen knives, you would not stop setting the boundary if they indicated "No" to you or that they wanted the knives back. In this case we have a different bigger picture, where their physical safety is more important. This is why it is important that we carefully consider each boundary we create and try to create as few as possible. We want to create an environment for our children where we can give control and say "Yes" to them 90 percent of the time and create boundaries 10 percent of the time.

How do I decide what is a boundary?

Most parents, like yourself, already have some boundaries you have set for your children. Moving forward, why not take some time to consider each particular boundary you create very carefully. With each boundary we are saying that stopping our children is, in that instant, more important than giving them control. With each boundary you create, ask yourself *Does this boundary aid my child's overall health and safety?* For example, making sure that your child does not drink the toilet water does. Making your child wear their hair a certain way every day may not be one, as it will not hurt your child or anyone else if they choose not to. This would be something that you can let go of and give your child control over.

The following exercise is to help you create your boundaries within your home in four different categories.

EXERCISE 2.1

Create boundaries around anything that could cause physical harm to your child, or to another person. Their safety is our number 1 priority. I would not watch a child play with something that could hurt them. I would not watch a child lean out of a window, or innocently put a rope around another child's neck to play horsey. We would of course stop our children from doing anything that could be physically harmful to themselves or others.

The lines provided below are for you to write down boundaries you would like to create for your child in this category. If you are a single parent then yippee!—only you have to agree on the boundaries you are going to set with your children. If you have a partner it is important that you do this exercise with them, so that they agree with the boundaries, and are also prepared to follow through with setting them.

_____

_____

_____

_____

_____

_____

_____

_____

_____

_____

_____

When you have written your list, go back and see if you can cross one or more off your list by eliminating the situation. For example, if your child likes to lean out of the window you could always lock all the windows so that your child does not have the opportunity to do this.

Create boundaries around taking care of objects. This would mean not sitting back and watching our children rip a book to pieces, or draw all over our walls. Giving control does not mean that you watch as your children dismantle every lamp you have or spin your precious CDs until they are unusable. *Your child is intelligent and can learn what they can and cannot play with.*

The lines provided below are for you to write down boundaries in this category you would like to create for your child. When you have written your list, go back and see if you can cross one or more off your list by eliminating the situation. For example, if your child likes to rip your books, put them in a place where they cannot reach them.

_____

_____

_____

_____

_____

_____

_____

_____

_____

_____

_____

_____

_____

Create boundaries around hygiene. This would mean not letting your child put their hands down the toilet, eat their diapers, or other people's plasters, and so forth.

The lines provided below are for you to write down boundaries in this category you would like to create for your child. When you have written your list, go back and see if you can cross one or more off your list by eliminating the situation. For example, you could get a lock for the toilets in your house, so that your child cannot play in them when you are not around.

_____

_____

_____

Create boundaries around when their bedtime is. You are the boss when it comes to bedtime. Again, I know that some of you may feel like your child will just not go to sleep and do not know how to encourage them to do so. Chapter 10 will help you with this and gives many concrete suggestions on how to do this. For now write down what time you would want your child to go to sleep. The first step will be to begin with the idea that you can decide what you want. How to get there will be discussed in chapter 10.

The lines provided below are for you to write down what time you want your child to go to sleep or stay in their room.

_____

_____

_____

_____

•••••••••••••

THE ATTITUDE OF BOUNDARY SETTING

Be loving, not punitive. It is tempting sometimes to feel that if our children have done something "wrong" we must correct them, and we can do so in a critical or punishing way. See it instead as a chance to express our love to our child. This boundary is a chance to help our child learn how to take care of themselves, others, and their environment. It is a useful, necessary, and wonderful opportunity to share some important knowledge with our child. When we think of it that way we are more likely to approach it in an easy, kind, and non-judgmental way. Our child is then more likely to understand that we are not just stopping them from doing something they were interested in, but we are trying to help them with something.

Be consistent. Know the specific reasons for setting a particular boundary. This helps us really stand behind it so that we do not waver or decide that today it does not matter. Consistency is the key to setting any boundary. If we are not consistent then our children will most likely push that boundary. What creates a boundary is our determination around it.

Be unmovable. Commit to following through with setting your boundary.

Harry, a four-year-old with autism, wanted to drink the water in the toilet bowl. As a way to keep him safe I sat on the toilet seat for 45 minutes. Harry tried many tactics to get me off that seat. He wanted to get me off so that he could drink the toilet water again. I knew that I was doing the most loving thing I could by helping him understand that the toilet water was not healthy to drink. I was being "unmovable" in that I knew that there was nothing he could do that would make me get off and let him do this potential harmful act. He spent 45 minutes kicking me, trying to pull or push me off, slapping me, pulling my hair, and screaming "off" at the top of his lungs. While he tried the above things with all his might I held two major beliefs that helped me stay the course with this very persistent little man: "There is nothing more important for me to be doing right now than setting this very useful boundary for Harry." "Setting this boundary with Harry is a way of loving him and letting him know what is healthy and what is not." He did stop trying and went to play with some books in the playroom. By sitting it out and staying longer than him, I communicated to him that I was prepared to follow through with the boundaries I created, no matter what he did in response. He therefore learned that he could trust my boundaries and what I said to him. He never tried to drink the toilet water with me present again.

COMMUNICATE YOUR BOUNDARIES TO YOUR CHILD AHEAD OF TIME

It is useful to explain what the boundaries are ahead of time, whether your child is not yet verbal or can talk fluently. Explain the new situation to them so that when you begin to put them into action they will not come as a complete surprise.

If your child is yet to be verbal, take advantage of the time when they sit in your lap or on the sofa beside you, or maybe while they are sitting down and eating, or in the bathtub, to explain a couple of the new boundaries. If you have decided to create five new boundaries, explain each new one, one at a time.

If your child can talk, choose a time when they are not verbally stimming/isming, maybe when you are walking somewhere together or in the car.

As we speak of the new boundaries it's important to explain all the reasons behind them, and that this is a way of taking care of them and helping them to be safe and healthy. It is essential that our children understand that we are taking care of them and not just deciding arbitrarily what they can or cannot do.

For example, when setting a boundary of "you cannot jump on the trampoline if you have food in your mouth" you could say: "I know that you would like to jump, but you have food in your mouth. Jumping with food in your mouth may cause you to choke. Which will mean that your food may get stuck in your throat and then you would not be able to breathe. As a way to help you I am going to put the trampoline away while you eat. Once you have finished eating then you can jump all you want. I just want to keep you as safe as possible."

HOW TO SET A BOUNDARY

When we are setting a boundary it is because we are taking care of our children, making sure that they are safe. I am going to illustrate how to set a boundary using the example of setting the boundary of "not putting your hands down the toilet."

1. **Explain while taking action.** You might say something like "The toilet water is full of germs, so I am taking your hands out of the toilet so that you do not get sick." Do this with a loving and calm tone while you are actually physically taking their hands out of the toilet.

2. **Make sure that they cannot do it again.** Take care of the environment so that it is not easy for them to do it again immediately. You can do this by either standing in front of

the object so that they cannot get to it, or if possible, move it out of reach. Obviously we cannot put the toilet out of reach, but we can put the toilet seat down and sit on it so that they cannot put their hands in it again. Do this in a quick, easy, and loving way. Remembering that setting the boundary is really useful for our children will help us do it with comfort and a smile on our faces. This will communicate to our children that we are helping them do something new and not that they have done something bad.

3. **Offer an alternative.** We want to show our children that we are helpful. The Son-Rise Program describes this as the principle of being "User-Friendly." A way to be "User-Friendly" is to offer an alternative. This way we show our children that we understand they want to do something, that it matters to us, and we will help them find a safe way to do it. This will help our children come to us when they want something. The more our children see us as useful, the more they will move toward us and the more opportunities we will have to teach them the life skills outlined in this book. In order to offer an alternative, we have to know what it is that our children want, so take a moment and think about the activity they are doing and what they are getting from it. In the example of putting hands in the toilet, our child wants to engage with water, so we can help them understand that they can play with the water in the sink but not in the toilet. Offer them the alternative of playing with the water in the sink.

   If your child likes to rip books, after explaining to them that we want to keep the books whole so that they can enjoy them later, we can offer our child some paper to rip instead. That way we can keep the books intact and our children can enjoy the activity they were seeking. If our children want to play with a bottle of pills, liking the sound as they shake the bottle, offer them another bottle and fill it with rice that will make a similar sound as they shake it. That way your child gets to play and be safe at the same time.

4. **Be unmovable.** See it through to the end. No matter how our child responds to our boundary setting, it is vital to be brave enough to never waver in our conviction. This is one

of the reasons why it is so important to carefully pick what boundaries we want to set. This way we know clearly that it is one we really intend to follow through.

Our children may try to talk us out of setting the boundary by telling us how they really need to do the activity or to have the object. I have had children tell me that I was mean, or that they will die if I do not let them dismantle the air-conditioning system. One very cheeky boy told me that his life was not worth living anymore because I did not let him draw Charlie Brown on our playroom wall with a black marker. Just 30 minutes later he was drawing Charlie Brown on a poster board instead, happy as a lamb. Another little girl told me very politely, "Kate, you are being ridiculous, my mom lets me do this all the time." Eating markers—hmmmm, I did not think so.

For our children who are not yet verbal they may cry in an attempt to communicate to us that they really, really want to do what it is that we are setting a boundary around. They may keep throwing our hands up to the place where the markers are so that they can draw on the walls. They may hit, bite, spit, and much more. This is what they are supposed to do, figure out what they can do to get us to let them do what they want. This is the time for us to really take ownership of being the adult with the bigger picture, and not give in to our children wanting immediate gratification.

We can do this by telling them that even if they do these things we will still set the boundary, because we love them and want to keep them safe and sound. Go the distance. It may take a while for some boundaries to be set, but once our children know that we mean business we will most likely not have to set it again. If our children try to push the boundary in the ways described above, try to remain calm and easy. A thought that will help us do this is: *There is nothing more important for me to do with my child right now than to set this boundary; however long it takes, it will be useful for my child to learn.*

Their job is to push the boundary—our job is to hold it firm for them.

TROUBLESHOOTING

? *My child will chew on everything, even the woodwork in my house; this is not good for her teeth and I am afraid she will get a splinter. How do I set a boundary around this when the woodwork is all over the house?*

Give an alternative—get a big box filled with toys that she can chew on. You can buy some great chew toys for your child (e.g. online at www.arktherapeutic.com). Have a chew toy available in each room of your house, or tie a chew toy around their neck like a necklace; that way it will always be available when you need to give an alternative.

Each time your child goes to chew on the wood, gently and quickly move them away from the wood and offer them a chew toy instead. Experiment with different chew toys until you get the one that your child enjoys the most. If they chew on wood then most likely they would like a hard chew toy. Make this exchange each time they chew on the wood; be consistent with setting this boundary and giving the alternative. If you are consistent with this, no matter how many times you have to do it, they will get the message and most likely start to seek the stimulation from the chew toy instead of the wood.

? *My child spits on the window and plays with it with her finger drawing patterns. Do I set a boundary around this?*

This is where I would advise you to consider each boundary you want to set with care. Your child spitting and playing with her saliva on the window does not harm the window, or your child, or anyone else. It does not pose a health risk, so therefore it does not seem necessary. This may be a boundary that you would want to set with your typical child, but I would not suggest it for your child with autism. With our children on the autism spectrum we want to set the least number of new boundaries possible. This means that we can still create an environment where our children see us as helpful people to interact with rather than people who are constantly stopping them from doing things that are important to them.

? *My child likes to play with our bottle of dishwashing detergent. When she has it I offer my child an alternative by giving her an empty bottle to play with but she will not let go of the bottle of detergent I do not want her to play with. What do I do then?*

If your child has an object that you do not want them to have because it is not safe for them or they could break it, swop it for an object that they can have. For instance, in this case they have a bottle of detergent, and you are swopping it with an empty plastic bottle. When you do the swop, the key is to do it quickly before your child has a chance to hold on tightly. If your child does hold on to the object, do not get into a fight and push and pull with them, as this will just make it more exciting for your child to hold on. Instead, hold on to the object you want to exchange and move in the direction your child is pulling that object. This takes the fight out of the situation. While you are doing this say to your child some version of: "I am going to hold on to this until you are ready to let go of it. It is too dangerous for you to have, as the contents of this bottle could make you sick if you ate it." Then keep hold of it and move in the direction your child is pulling the bottle. This means your child may walk around holding the detergent, with you attached to the detergent bottle, for a few minutes—as soon as your child lets go, you remove the object. Without the added fight element your child will soon become bored and let go. Once they have let go, praise them and give them the alternative.

I have used this technique with children at the Autism Treatment Center of America countless times—it's a gem!

? *My child likes to draw on the walls. I have done what you suggest by giving her an alternative of drawing on paper, which she accepts some of the time; other times when she gets hold of a pen she ignores my offer of drawing on the paper and will draw on the wall. What do I do?*

There are two ways to think about this situation:

- It could be a "button push," which means that your child may be drawing on the wall at times just to get a reaction from you. For example, they may know that you do not want them to do it and want to see what you will do. For instance, some of us will raise our voices, or talk in a high squeaky voice, when telling our children not to do something. One sign to look for when determining whether she is "button pushing" is to look and see if she is looking at you as she is drawing on the wall. This is usually an indication that she is more interested in seeing your reaction than she is in drawing on the wall itself. If this is the case, I would suggest that you read Chapter 6 on "button pushing," which will tell you in detail what to do when your child is doing this.

- It could be that is just too irresistible for her. If you have done all the above suggestions and ruled out "button pushing" then it is most likely something she is just too fascinated by. We could reason with her all we like but she may just feel that she "needs" to do this activity and for some reason that it is useful to her. If this is the case, I would just not make the pens available to her until a day comes when she can use pens without the urge to draw on the walls. I would suggest that you do not have any markers in the house; or if you have other children who will want to use markers that you have a very special place for them that your child with autism does not have access to. When your other children want to use markers make sure that they do so when your child with autism is not in the same room. I would also suggest that you be careful where you put your pens. Make sure that you put them in a special place for you and your partner and you get used to putting them back in this place. Then I would suggest that you experiment every three months or so by offering your child with autism some markers and paper to draw on and asking her to draw on the paper. As she grows, her ability to follow through with not drawing on the walls may change.

BOUNDARY SETTING ACTION CHECKLIST

☐ Limit your boundaries to as few as possible.

☐ Create boundaries around the following:

   ☐ Create boundaries for things that could be harmful to your child.

   ☐ Create boundaries for things that are dangerous for your child to do.

☐ Create boundaries for things that are not healthy or hygienic for your child to do.

☐ Create a united front. Have everyone who interacts with your child know what boundaries to create and how to do this.

☐ Explain to your child the boundaries you have created ahead of time.

☐ Explain to your child that you are setting the boundary to take care of them and be helpful to them.

☐ See the boundary as a loving act, not punitive.

☐ When setting the boundary, consider the following:

  ☐ Be loving and caring in your tone and actions.

  ☐ Explain to them what you are doing and why.

  ☐ Be consistent.

  ☐ Be unmovable—see it through to the end.

  ☐ Create it so they can't do it straight away again. For instance, if they have just put their hands down the toilet, sit on the toilet seat.

  ☐ Give them an alternative. For instance, if they were ripping a book, give them some paper for them to rip instead.

Chapter 3

BELIEVE IN YOUR CHILD'S ABILITY TO LEARN

I know that you believe in your child. You are at this moment reading a book in the hope that it will help you to help your child. You would not be doing so if you did not believe that your child could learn and grow. This is one of the most powerful things you can do for your child. It is this belief that will keep you trying. This belief will fuel your actions and what you offer your child. As you embark on this journey with your child, hold this belief close to your heart. Keep it beating strong and vibrant. Never let anyone try and convince you otherwise. As your child's parent you are their most important advocate, their most important cheerleader and coach. Believe that it is possible for your child to gain the skills discussed in this book, such as:

- becoming toilet trained

- enjoying brushing their teeth

- getting dressed by themselves in the morning

- learning to be gentle with others

- sleeping through the night

- using clear words and gestures to communicate (versus the tantrum)

- eating new foods.

Maybe some of you have certain doubts about your child's ability to learn one or more of the skills listed above. Often when parents have doubts, they usually share with me that it's because they have not seen any evidence yet that their child will be able to do the skill.

However, what our children are currently doing need not be a template for what they will or won't do in the future.

Let's look at the concept of belief. We believe all sorts of things without seeing the outcome first. We plant seeds believing that that particular seed will grow and flourish before it actually has. This belief supports us in watering them and making sure they get enough sun to flourish and grow. When our children are babies we believe that one day they will walk, so we support them by holding their hands and encourage them to take their first step. Just because our children have been diagnosed with autism does not mean that they cannot grow and flourish and reach their full potential. It just means that they learn differently than their typical peers. This belief is the guiding-force that will help us try for them. No child learns completely by themselves; adults give them opportunities and encouragement. Our children have to try harder and it may take them longer to learn some skills than their neuro-typical peers, but that does not mean that they cannot learn just as well. *Let's not look at what our children are doing today to dictate what they will be doing in the future.*

During the Son-Rise Program Intensive we are often asked by parents to work on different self-help skills. One particular week we were asked to help a little boy called Karim learn to brush his teeth. So the staff enthusiastically created games and opportunities for Karim to want to clean his teeth. It was the fourth day, and we had given Karim many opportunities to clean his teeth; we had persisted and made it fun. Although Karim had watched us and smiled as we excitedly encouraged him, he had not actually cleaned his teeth. His mom told me that she wanted us to stop trying as it was obvious to her that he could not or would not do this. Her reasoning was that if he could he would have done so by now. I was in the middle of asking her why she believed this when one of our staff child facilitators came in and told us with great excitement that Karim had just picked up a toothbrush and put it in his mouth. Yeah for Karim!

Karim's mom did what we all often do—she created a timeframe— and then when that timeframe was up she decided that he was not going to do it. One thing we don't know is how long it is going to take for our children to acquire these skills. One thing we do know is if we stop believing in the possibility we will give up and then there is no chance they ever will. *Focus on what you want for your children and give them the opportunities to get there.*

RE-EXAMINE WHAT YOU THINK YOUR CHILD IS CAPABLE OF

Take a moment to reflect. When you talk about your child do you start a sentence with the following:

- He can't...

- He won't...

- He doesn't...

I am sure that you will probably find that you do; all of us do at some point. There is nothing wrong with this. Perhaps what you are saying is currently true about your child. However, the important thing here is to keep checking in with our children to see if this is still the case. What they can or can't do yesterday doesn't necessarily have anything to do with what they can or can't do today.

One parent I worked with was amazed that her child put on his sweater by himself. When I gave him the chance to put on the sweater himself he did. His mom did not believe he could do this, thus never gave him the opportunity.

Another mom was equally amazed that her child ate his apple sauce with a spoon. I had simply given him the spoon, when he did not take it from me I explained how it would be fun to use the spoon because then he could keep his fingers clean. After I explained this he took the spoon and used it. His mom shared with me that it never crossed her mind that he could do it as he had not done it before, and so she had not asked him to.

These are just two examples where our children's capabilities were not realized because the adults in their lives did not believe they could be a possibility. This is why it is exciting to re-examine what we think our children are capable of.

You as the parent know the most about your children. You have the most experience and depth of knowledge of your child. For example:

- the color he prefers

- the food he will eat

- the songs he will sing with you

- the fact that he will not let you play with puppets

- the fact that he bursts into tears every time you sing "Happy Birthday"

- the fact that he will run and hide or put his hand over your mouth when you talk loudly

- the fact that he does not play with toys, preferring to play with pieces of string, and tapping with his fingers on the floor and walls.

You know this because you have seen so much concrete evidence of it time after time. If you experience your child never allowing you to play with puppets, I think that is evidence enough to say that at this moment in time it is a correct observation. But it is not written in stone. What is important is to check in with your child periodically to see if the puppet situation still stands. Maybe it was a correct observation six months ago, but your child has now moved on and now likes you to play with puppets, but because you never questioned this old observation you have not tried to do it in six months. Not questioning our observations of our children can lead us to miss out on new opportunities for learning and growth. Instead of saying:

- He can't...

- He won't...

- He doesn't...

practice saying:

- My child is getting ready to...

Leave the door open so that he can start doing it at any moment. Then we may start to give him more opportunities to do so, and start looking for it. Remember that our children are listening to what we are saying. You may have noticed that I refer to a certain population of our children as being "not verbal yet" instead of the more traditional phrase "nonverbal." This is because it more accurately describes our children. When we label them as "nonverbal" we are suggesting that they will always be that way. I just don't believe that. Our children are forever evolving and changing.

EXERCISE 3.1

On the lines provided below write a list of ten things you observe about your child, and in the next couple of weeks check out each of these observations and see if they are still true. Get in the habit of doing this on a monthly basis. That way you will be up to date and more current about what your child is willing to try, experience, and do.

1. _____

   _____

2. _____

   _____

3. _____

   _____

4. _____

   _____

5. _____

   _____

6. _____

   _____

7. _____

   _____

8. _____

   _____

9. _____

   _____

10. _____

    _____

·················

Chapter 4

MOTIVATION: THE KEY TO EVERYTHING

Motivation is the key to everything. We work harder, learn quicker, and engage more when we are really interested and enjoying what we are doing. Raun K. Kaufman, in his book *Autism Breakthrough: The Groundbreaking Method That Has Helped Families All Over the World,* says:

> Motivation is the engine of growth. It is the single largest factor in your child's learning and progress. When a child is following his or her own intrinsic interests and motivations, learning comes fast and furious. (Kaufman 2014)

I worked with Gabriella, a beautiful young girl of seven. Gabriella loved food—she wanted to eat and look at pictures of food all day long. At that time food was her one and only motivation. Because Gabriella focused nearly all of her attention around food, her parents were trying to move her away from food and get her into doing something else. They wanted her to read, learn math, and experience more of what "the world had to offer." They did this by introducing subjects and things that had nothing to do with food. This was not working. She showed no interest in what they were offering her. This was because they were completely ignoring what it was that she enjoyed—food.

The idea is to use your child's motivations, by marrying the goal or skill you want your child to learn with what it is they enjoy. We did that with Gabriella. So instead of trying to get her away from the subject of food we embraced it and made it the central focus of everything we offered her. Over the next two years she learned to speak through naming all the different foods. She learned math by cooking her favorite foods and measuring out the ingredients. She learned to be flexible and spontaneous by making up her own recipes. She learned about the different cultures of the world through studying their different foods. She even learned French and Italian!

It is important to note that this is not about giving rewards for a job well done. *It is about putting what they enjoy at the center of the activity or learning.* This is going to be so important as you go about encouraging your child to do all the skills outlined in this book.

Carl was ten years old and he loved staccato rhythms. He would tap out rhythms using his fingers on the floor, the walls, and the backs of books. His preferred state of being was to lie on a beanbag and tap out rhythms. One goal we worked on with him was to encourage him to be more active. So I brought in a skipping rope. Instead of introducing it to him in a traditional way I showed him how he could use the skipping rope in a way that I knew would interest him first. I took the handles of the skipping rope and tapped out a rhythm. I then gave it to him and he tapped out a rhythm. Then I swung the skipping rope in a way that the rope made a rhythm on the floor. This helped him become interested and interact with the skipping rope. We had a lot of fun, and by the end of the session he had attempted to skip. Hooray for Carl! Putting what he was motivated for at the center of the activity helped him reach the goal of being more active.

FIND OUT WHAT MOTIVATES YOUR CHILD

We can find out what really motivates our children by observing where they put their attention. Then we can marry their motivation with the goal we have for our child. This book is about how to help our children with their self-help skills, such as taking a bath, sitting on the toilet, eating new foods, and much more. These endeavors will be so much more successful if we do them in a way that interests our children. For some of you it will be immediately obvious to you what motivates your child; for others it may not be so apparent. The exercise below is designed to help you find out what motivates your child.

EXERCISE 4.1

Spend 15 minutes a day for five days just observing your child as they play by themselves. Notice not just what they are playing with but how they are playing with it. What senses are they

predominantly using? As you observe them, notice what they are
doing; if they are tapping things with their fingers then that is their
motivation. It does not have to be playing with something in the
traditional sense. Our children play and explore differently. The
following list will help you observe in a particular way. Just tick the
boxes that are relevant to your child.

He touches or taps things in a rhythmic way.

- ☐ The rhythm is fast.
- ☐ The rhythm is slow.
- ☐ The rhythm is staccato.
- ☐ The rhythm is syncopated.

Add your child's rhythm on the lines provided below.

_____

_____

_____

_____

She is visually stimulated.

- ☐ She looks at things out of the corner of her eye.
- ☐ She lines things up in neat rows.
- ☐ She likes to arrange things in scenes.
- ☐ She likes to arrange things in piles.
- ☐ She stares at the wall or ceiling, or at the woodwork or light switches.
- ☐ She stares intently at her own fingers as she slowly wiggles them.
- ☐ She looks at patterns while running her fingers over the pattern.
- ☐ She will watch the credits roll down the TV again and again.
- ☐ She will draw.
- ☐ She likes to watch the chalk dust fall.

☐ She watches things that move like fans or any electrical equipment.

☐ She stares at light on floorboards.

☐ She watches little things falling through the air like rice.

☐ She watches a scarf fall through the air.

☐ She closely watches the wheels of a car spin.

☐ She watches a piece of string dangle.

☐ She waves a belt along the floor, watching it move like a snake.

Add what your child watches and how on the lines provided below.

_____

_____

_____

_____

He likes to engage in physical activities.

☐ He runs from one side of the room to another banging his hands onto the walls.

☐ He paces using large steps, starting slowly and gathering speed, and then slowing down and again gathering speed.

☐ He flaps his hands, stimulating mainly his wrists.

☐ He flaps his fingers only.

☐ He shakes his head from side to side.

☐ He pushes his tongue against the side of his cheeks.

☐ He chews on any object he has.

☐ He slaps the side of his head and legs, or claps his hands.

☐ He jumps.

☐ He is constantly in motion.

☐ He holds an object most of the time.

Add your child's particular physical activity on the lines provided below.

_____

_____

_____

_____

She likes to listen to sounds.

- ☐ She puts a car up close to her ear and listens to the whirl of the car wheels.

- ☐ She makes sounds to herself as she jumps, spins, or watches things fall.

- ☐ She listens to the clank of a belt buckle falling to the ground as she watches it fall.

- ☐ She bangs doors, listening to the click of the door handle opening or closing.

- ☐ She says the same phrase or word over and over again, with a particular inflection or rhythm.

- ☐ She shakes bells.

Add the specific sound your child likes to hear on the lines below.

_____

_____

_____

_____

He likes patterns.

- ☐ He likes to do puzzles.

- ☐ He likes numbers.

- ☐ He likes to spell words.

- ☐ He likes to solve math problems.

On the lines below write your child's own specific interest in patterns.

_____

_____

_____

_____

She likes to engage with textures and touch.

- ☐ She loves soft things.
- ☐ She loves hard and bumpy textures.
- ☐ She loves furry things.
- ☐ She likes sandpaper.
- ☐ She will wrap herself up in a blanket.
- ☐ She loves silky cloths.
- ☐ She will roll cars up and down her arms.
- ☐ She likes soft touch.
- ☐ She likes hard pressure like squeezes.
- ☐ She loves ribbon.
- ☐ She loves the feel of hair.

On the lines below write any other texture or touch your child likes.

_____

_____

_____

_____

What kind of spaces does he like?

- ☐ He likes the doors and windows to be open.
- ☐ He will always close the door.
- ☐ He will surround himself with cushions.
- ☐ He will play underneath the table, or in a small play tent or play house.

☐ He will play surrounded by a fortress of books or stuffed animals.

☐ He likes to play in a dark space.

☐ He likes to play in a light space.

On the lines provided below write down any other kind of space your child enjoys.

_____

_____

_____

_____

What type of characters does she like?

☐ She likes plastic Disney characters.

☐ She likes soft plush Disney characters.

☐ She likes movie characters.

☐ She likes characters from a storybook.

Write your childs favorite characters on the lines provided below.

_____

_____

_____

_____

What music or song does your child like?
Write them down on the lines provided below.

_____

_____

_____

_____

Does your child show you a color preference?
If so, write them down on the lines provided below.

_____

_____

_____

_____

•••••••••••••

EXERCISE 4.2
••

This time notice how your child responds to what *you* do. As you read the list below see if your child likes you to do any of the actions. If you are not sure, then find out by trying the action with your child. If they do, then that's their motivation.

- ❐ Speaking in funny voices, like Mickey Mouse and Donald Duck
- ❐ Using slapstick humor like pretending to fall on a banana skin
- ❐ Big gestures, and big facial expressions
- ❐ Big celebrations
- ❐ Singing to them
- ❐ Playing musical instruments
- ❐ Dancing in big and funny ways
- ❐ Whispering
- ❐ Using anticipation
- ❐ Talking softly
- ❐ Clapping hands
- ❐ Pretending to be an animal
- ❐ Reading books out loud
- ❐ Tickling her
- ❐ Big squeezes
- ❐ Blowing on her body

Add any other things that you do that motivate your child on the lines provided below.

_____

_____

_____

_____

_____

_____

• • • • • • • • • • • •

Now you have just created a list of your child's own unique motivations. As you read the upcoming chapters use these specific motivations to encourage your child to want to achieve the goals in this book, by putting your child's motivation at the center of the activity. An example follows:

Marcus's story: goal = eat new foods; motivation = Spider-Man

Marcus was five and completely in love with Spider-Man. I think the only clothes he ever wore while I knew him was a Spider-Man costume—so cute! While he loved Spider-Man he seemed not to be so interested in eating. He was underweight and his parents were understandably concerned about his health. So we took his motivation for Spider-Man and married it with our goal of wanting him to eat. We started by making up stories about what Spider-Man loved to eat after he had done his day's work of being a super hero. Marcus was amazing at drawing, so we drew cartoons together about Spider-Man, and every place we could we would draw Spider-Man eating, or stopping off at the shops to get his favorite foods. These were of course all the different foods that we wanted Marcus to eat. We would then bring in what we started to call "Spider-Man Meals." We introduced the food on Spider-Man party plates, and while we were playing we would stop for a Spider-Man Munch. Within a couple of weeks Marcus had started to put on weight. This was because we made eating the most interesting we could for him by putting what he enjoyed most at the center of the activity.

Enjoy!

Chapter 5

TALK TO YOUR CHILDREN: THE POWER OF THE EXPLANATION

Two things to believe about your children:

- They are intelligent.

- They can listen and understand what we say to them.

These two beliefs, if you choose to adopt them, will profoundly impact you and your child's future. It will affect the way that you implement every single suggestion in this book. It will also make it easier for your child to learn and attempt to do all the skills discussed in this book.

For those of you who have highly verbal children, these statements may be obvious. For those of you whose children are partially or not verbal yet, these statements may be groundbreaking. If they are, I am excited for you! If you can believe these two statements about your child, it will change everything for the two of you. There is nothing to lose and everything to gain.

YOUR CHILD IS INTELLIGENT

This belief is paramount to the success of your child. Why? There have been studies suggesting that our belief in a child's intelligence can have a direct effect on whether that child succeeds or fails. This is called the "Pygmalion effect" or "Rosenthal effect." "When we expect certain behaviors of others, we are likely to act in ways that make the expected behavior more likely to occur" (Rosenthal and Jacobson 1968).

Rosenthal predicted that when given the information that certain students had higher IQs than others, elementary school teachers may unconsciously behave in ways that facilitate and encourage the students' success. "In terms of teaching, faculty who gripe about students establish a climate of failure, but faculty who value their students' abilities create a climate of success" (Rosenthal and Babad 1985). This shows us that the way that we think and the things that we believe about our children affect the way that we approach them and deal with them every day.

Most of us have seen our children show great intelligence and understanding of what is going on around them. Sam is a great example of this. He accessed his parents' computer and successfully bought tickets to "Legoland." To do this he had to use his parents' credit card; this included turning the card over and typing in the security number! At this time Sam was only seven years old and not yet speaking. This was the first time his parents realized he could read. I have worked with children who, although they have not demonstrated an ability to speak, are able to pick the most complicated locks and do 10,000-piece puzzles without even looking at the pieces. All of this takes great intelligence.

Close your eyes for a moment and think of all the things that your child does that demonstrates their intelligence. Or things that you have seen your child do that surprised you, and you found yourself thinking, "I didn't know he could do that." These are signs of your child's sometimes hidden intelligence.

YOUR CHILD LISTENS AND CAN UNDERSTAND WHAT YOU SAY

In the late 1800s when cerebral palsy was first categorized as a diagnosis, it was thought that it was accompanied with mental retardation. Now it is known as a physical illness only. The Early Childhood Initiative Foundation states: "By definition, having cerebral palsy doesn't tell us anything about a child's ability to learn and reason. How much and how fast they learn may be different from child to child." (Early Childhood Initiative Foundation.)

Professionals working in this field know that it is the inability to control facial muscles that results in a child profoundly affected by cerebral palsy being unable to speak. This alone is not a sign of lack of intelligence or their inability to understand what is said to them.

I do not think that it is much different with children on the autism spectrum. They are often so preoccupied with dealing with their own sensory systems that they cannot always show us that they understand what we are saying. Many women who have given birth have described how they ignored the people around them during the process of giving birth. The birth experience being so intense, it is impossible to focus their attention on responding. This is of course not because they did not understand what was being asked, but because they were immersed in doing something that demanded their whole attention. It can be like that for our children. *The challenge our children have is showing us a response that we can understand. A lack of response does not mean a lack of understanding.*

Today there is an ever-growing body of evidence of children who cannot respond verbally or physically to their parents' requests, or events going on around them, who demonstrate through typing without assistance that they are aware of everything and have thoughts, observations, and desires for their lives. Carly is a great example of this (see her story at www.youtube.com/watch?v=vNZVV4Ciccg). When asked to contribute to her Grade 10 Individualized Education Plan she answered the question "Is there any additional information you would like to share that you feel it is important we know?" as follows: "That I am eager to learn and that even if I am not looking at you, I am still listening and paying attention" (Fleischmann 2012).

Naoki Higashida is a young man with autism who also communicates through typing independently. In his book *The Reason I Jump* he answers the question "Do you find childish language easier to understand?" as follows:

> Children with autism are also growing and developing every single day, yet we are forever being treated like babies. I guess it is because we seem to act younger than our true age, but whenever someone treats me as if I'm still a toddler, it really hacks me off. I don't know whether people think I'll understand baby language better, or whether they think I just prefer being spoken to in that way. I'm not asking you to deliberately use difficult language when you talk to people with autism—just that you treat us as we are, according to our age. Every single time I'm talked down to, I end up feeling utterly miserable—as if I'm being given zero change of a decent future. (Higashida 2013)

Your child does listen to what you say. Your child can understand what you say to them. Your child is intelligent. This has been my everyday experience as I work with children on the autism spectrum. I remember working with a beautiful three-year-old boy for a total of 15 hours, of which for at least 13 of those hours he was engaged in staring at and touching the fringe of a pink blanket, rarely engaging with me. I so enjoyed playing with him and Joining him in his activities of looking at and touching the pink fringe. At that time he spoke only three clear words and his interactive attention span was two minutes. His parents ran a full-time Son-Rise Program for him at home and I worked with him again a year and a half later. I was excited to meet him again and he had developed hugely. He could talk and have conversations, and his interactive attention span was now 20 minutes. A far cry from the little boy I first met. Within the first 20 minutes of playing with me he proceeded to tell me in great detail everything that he and I had done 18 months earlier, and all the things I had said to him. At that time he had not been able to show me that he was taking in what I was saying to him, but obviously he had. He was also demonstrating a magnificent memory.

Can you believe that your child can understand you even if they do not display the type of clear evidence in the examples above? Can you take a leap of faith? I ask you, why not? There is no downside to this. It will not hurt your child in any way. It will only open up doors and create understanding for your child and help you work together in harmony. It is my experience that the more fully we explain what is going on and really talk to our children on the autism spectrum, the more they work with us and become open to our direction.

VERBALLY EXPLAIN EVERYTHING IN DETAIL TO YOUR CHILD

In order to participate in the world, we need to understand what is going on in our environment and what's happening. For example, making transitions with our children from one place to another can be very difficult. Would you not be a little resistant if you did not know where you were going or why? Our children are carted around from place to place. From school to therapy; from home to the doctor's; and to the pool and back again. Do they know where they are going? When they are put in the car, is it to Grandma's where they love swinging on her swing, or to the hospital where the lights are too bright and the sound too chaotic for their over-sensitive ears? At least when the school bus arrives it is clear to them where they are going! Giving our children clear verbal explanations at their current age level will help them understand what is happening and what is going to happen.

Clear verbal explanations will help our children to want to take any type of medication, supplements, or vitamins we may want them to take. Do they know how helpful this is to them and how it will aid their bodies? Do we let them know, or are we sneakily trying to get it in them without telling them what we are up to? Let them know that the medicine that you want to give them will take away the pain that they are feeling and help them be well.

Clear explanations will help our children understand that we care. If we do not explain why we are telling them "No" to something that they want, then how are they supposed to know that we have their very best interests at heart? For example, let your child know that if he eats that eighth cookie he will most likely have an upset stomach and be sick, and that you are loving him and taking care of him by not letting him have it. Or that they cannot go outside because it is raining, and if they get wet they may get a cold, and not be able to do the things that they love to do, like running and jumping. When we explain things to our children we give them the chance to know that we are on their side and are helping them.

When you explain the why, what, and how of things *in detail* you will most likely find that your children will comply more and resist less. Below is a list of things that would be useful to explain to your children. This is just a starter list; not everything is listed below, just a few suggestions so you get the idea.

- When you are going to leave the house let them know the day's events in the morning, and then remind them 15 minutes before you are going to leave. Tell them:

  ○ Where you are going.

  ○ How long you will stay there.

  ○ If you are going to more than one place, in what order you will be visiting each place.

  ○ Why you are going there; if it is shopping that you will buy food for the week, or just milk. Or if it is to see Grandma that you are going to celebrate her birthday, or you need to talk to her, etc. Do tell them the real reason, however mundane or simple it sounds to you.

    o What will happen in detail when you get there. For example, will there be other people at Grandma's? Will people be watching TV or having a meal together? If so, what will your child be most likely eating? Will there be a lot of noise? Does your child have to stay with the group or can he go off and play by himself in another room? Basically everything that is happening.

- That you are going to change their clothes.

- They are going to have a bath.

- Why they need to brush their teeth.

- Why they go to any therapy they do. If it is speech therapy, why it is helpful for them to learn to talk; if it is occupational therapy, why it is useful for them to move in the ways the therapist is asking them to.

- Why you do not want them to run in the car park, and what will happen to their bodies if a car hits them.

- Exactly how the medicine you are giving them will help their bodies. Use words that are age-appropriate for your child. If your child is a teenager or older, use the medical words or maybe even read the label out to them. If your child is three years old, use phrases that a three-year-old would understand.

When we do not believe that our children understand us we do not talk to them. When we do not talk to them they do not know what is going on. When we do not know what is going on we may become cautious about trusting those around us, and may even resist and refuse what is happening.

WHAT IF THEY DON'T UNDERSTAND?

If believing your child can understand you feels difficult, then consider the following. Even if a child does not understand every word it is still important to give clear, detailed explanations. When we listen to other people, we take in and understand what they are saying not just from the actual words themselves, but also from what is called a "feeling tone." A feeling tone is what we communicate by our tone of voice, our facial expressions, and our body language. That implies that our children do not have to understand every word to have sense of the meaning behind our words. As we are explaining to them how much we love them and enjoy them when they kiss and hug us, they pick up that we love them and enjoy them from the tone of our voice, our body language, and our facial expressions. If they do not understand everything but understand that we are here to help them, protect them, and are on their side, they will more likely trust us and go along with us, because we are communicating this to them. If we do not verbally communicate to them, then we are not passing this along.

Believe in your child's inner intelligence

Not only will giving your child clear explanations help your child understand the world around them, but also it will help them understand the good and wonderful intentions behind everything you are offering your child. Giving clear explanations to the children I work with has always brought me closer to them, and I have found them powerfully effective in creating a clear, strong, and trusting relationship with each child. Enjoy talking in more depth with your children. Never underestimate the power of an explanation.

TALKING TO YOUR CHILD ACTION CHECKLIST

☐ Believe that your child is intelligent.

☐ Believe that your child can listen and can understand what you say to them.

☐ Remember that a lack of response from your child does not mean a lack of understanding.

☐ Give clear verbal explanations to your child at their current age level.

☐ Explain to them their day, where they are going, and why.

☐ Explain to them what you are going to do before you do it. For example cleaning their teeth, brushing their hair, or putting on their jacket.

☐ Explain concepts to them. For example, why it is not useful for them to run in a car park, or why it is necessary for you to hold their hand as they cross the road.

Chapter 6
....

BUTTON PUSHING

Children are forever moving and interacting with their world. Everything is new for them and their job is to be curious, explore, and learn. Nothing is off limits. With this wonderful curiosity comes the desire for our children to button push. Button pushing refers to our children exploring our reactions to their behavior. What will we do if they do X? What will happen? Will it be fun? It is all about them finding out about us and the world around them, and how their actions affect their environment. We often give them good reason to continue to button push, because our reactions can be fun and amusing to watch. We may shout, jump up and down, speak in a high squeaky voice or turn red or stiff with rage. We can become as funny as watching a cartoon character.

When I was younger I knew exactly how to get an amusing reaction from my dad. I just had to get a fit of giggles at dinnertime and I would never be disappointed with his reaction. His face would stiffen, he would point his finger at me and talk in a stern voice, and start to threaten all sorts of consequences that I did not want, but I enjoyed the fact that I could invite such predictable behavior in him. The reaction I wanted was named "the wobble effect" by my sister and me. When he got angry his whole body would wobble, and whatever the consequences of my behavior I found this amusing enough to continue.

There are many ways that your child may button push. Crying and hitting are definitely two of them. I will talk about hitting and crying in the following two chapters. I have dedicated a separate chapter to each of those subjects. This chapter addresses the other varied things our children do to try and evoke our often very dramatic response. These include, but are not limited to the following:

- peeing on the floor instead of in the toilet

- drawing on the walls

- throwing their food

- spilling water

- spitting

- swearing

- picking their nose and eating it

- throwing a toy or breaking it

- twirling a finger through your hair

- poking at your breasts

- talking about a subject matter that people can find uncomfortable.

For example, I worked with a family who had a nine-year-old boy with autism. His whole family were vegans; they did not eat any animal products, and were very concerned for the welfare of animals. This little boy would love to talk about eating meat. He would talk about eating a "juicy steak of animal flesh" and lick his lips while looking intently at the reactions of his family. They were horrified, believing that they had failed to pass on their own values. They would gasp at his statements and shake their head, raising their voices as they lectured him about the welfare of animals. He did not want to eat meat; he just wanted to watch the horrified reactions of his family.

I worked with another boy who, due to his food allergies, was on a gluten-free and casein-free diet. He would tell his mom that he had just eaten gluten or casein. Then he would sit back and smile as she shouted and lectured him on how this was not a good thing. He actually never ate the food he was not allowed to eat—he just loved watching his mom's reaction.

Another child of five was more dramatic. Whenever he was in public and there was a baby, he would declare loudly so that everyone could hear, "That baby is ugly." You can imagine the discomfort and shocked faces that would arise from such a statement.

HOW TO IDENTIFY A BUTTON PUSH

If your child's attention is on you and you react to the activity, it is likely to be a button push. Look for the following signs:

- They look at you while they are doing the activity.

- They look at you right after they have done the activity.

- They announce to you that they have just done the activity.

- They smile or laugh when you react to what they have just done.

- They do it again right after you have asked them not to while looking at you.

Special note: If your child does an activity when they are by themselves—let's say they might be ripping paper or playing with water—they may be focusing very intensely on this activity and not noticing anyone around them. Even if when you see them doing it you give them a big reaction and say "No" to them, your reaction alone does not mean that it is a button push. If they were doing it by themselves then it is most likely one of their repetitive activities/isms/stims, and is not a button push. A button push is an activity your child does to get a reaction from another person—it is not something your child does when they are alone.

EXERCISE 6.1

Take a moment to think about your child. Think about anything they might do that you give a big reaction to. Now think about whether they seem interested in and are looking with amusement at your reaction. When you have done that write down your child's button-pushing behavior on the button pushing worksheet at the end of the chapter.

WHY DO OUR CHILDREN BUTTON PUSH?

- **It is fun!** It is as simple as that. We can be very entertaining for our children. Our reactions at times can be disproportionate to the actual actions of our children. All of us have experienced walking away from our children asking ourselves, "Why did I just react in that way?" It is this over-the-top reaction that our children start to look for again and again. As children, all of us have pushed other people's buttons too. Why? It can be very funny. Remember those long car trips as a child? Well, I remember one such trip when I was nine, where I found much-needed entertainment by pushing my sister's buttons. She did not want me to touch her while she was reading her book. Knowing this bothered her, I kept touching her shoulder with my finger. Each time I did this, or just pointed my finger in her direction, she would explode into high-pitch squeaky yelling. Which was met with my laughter.

- **It feels powerful.** When our children realize that they can create a reaction in us, not only is it fun, it gives them a sense of power and control in a world that they often experience as chaotic. Our children start to realize that they can now "make" another person react. Along with this new-found power comes a sense of control. When I do "X," Mom does "Y." Our children begin to think, "Ah ha, great! I can have an impact and control my world in this way." As we have discussed earlier, having control in their lives is very important for our children; thus button pushing can become another way to gain this control.

- **It could be a sign that they are becoming more interactive.** If you find that your child is suddenly going through a particularly intense period of button pushing it may be because they have become less exclusive and have grown in their interactive ability. When a child with autism becomes more aware of their environment they start to notice that what they do can cause another person to do something. If this is the case for your child, it is an exciting and important time of growth for them.

- **It could be a sign that they are under-stimulated.** If your child has increased their level of button pushing, it may be a sign that they are being under-stimulated. They are button pushing as a form of entertainment just because they have nothing better to do. Sometimes school programs or home-based programs can become stagnant. It may be that your child has grown, and needs more interesting and challenging activities and learning opportunities. Reassess your child's program to see if this is the case.

THREE EASY STEPS TO DEACTIVATE A BUTTON PUSH

• Change your internal reaction.

• Change your external reaction.

• React in a huge way to something you *do* want them to do.

Change your internal reaction

Our children button push to explore our reaction to their action. When our reaction is interesting to them then they will continue. The fastest way to stop your child from button pushing is to deactivate the button by changing your reaction. You want to do this on an internal level as well as on an external level. Many times parents tell me that they were furious with their children but that they managed not to show it. I have seen no successful way to do this. If you are actually furious then it will show on your face and in your body movement. Your body will stiffen, your eyes change, and your jaw tenses. Your children know you, and they know the difference between how you sound and behave when you are at ease and how you sound and behave when you are tense, uncomfortable, or annoyed. However much you may want to, there is no way of "fooling" them.

EXERCISE 6.2

Take a moment to think about what thoughts go through your mind when your child does this button-pushing behavior. Go to the button pushing worksheet at the end of the chapter and on the lines provided write down your internal feelings or thoughts when your child button pushes. If you are having difficulty coming up with an internal thought or feeling, read through the ones below to see if any of them sound familiar to you.

☐   I hate it when she does this.

☐   She is only doing this to bug me.

☐   I can't stand listening to this any longer.

☐   I just do not like it when she does this.

☐   I can't help it if I don't like bodily fluids.

☐   She should know better by now.

☐   She is just misbehaving.

....

Ok, so this is the really exciting part of this chapter—because you *can* change the way you are acting in relation to your child's button-pushing behaviors and then you *can* help them to find another way to behave; you have the power to make a difference by changing yourself first!

The first thing to do is: *internally relax.* Find a way to become relaxed with what your child is doing. You can do this by softening the thoughts you have about the action your child is doing.

If they are spilling water on the floor, you could soften your thoughts about it by thinking to yourself something like "It is not the end of the world—it can be tidied up."

If they are talking to you about a particular subject that you have found uncomfortable, or maybe they are telling you that they are going to throw all their toys out of the window, soften your thoughts about it by reminding yourself that they are saying this not because they believe it or will do it but because they want to see your reaction.

If they are screaming in a high-pitch way that you have previously found hard to listen to, soften your thoughts about it by reminding yourself that this sound will not go on forever, and that your child is doing this just to get a reaction. Embrace the sound and tap your toe to its rhythm; yes, you can do that. By relaxing into the sound and embracing it you will be more likely not to overreact and will be one step closer to not hearing it again.

Let that be your incentive. The more you can soften your thoughts about the action your child is doing, the easier it will be to change your reaction. Then it is more likely that your child will lose interest in doing the action.

Change your external reaction
EXERCISE 6.3
• •

Take a moment to think about what your reaction is to your child's
button push. What does your voice sound like? How do you move
your body? Go to the button pushing worksheet on at the end of the
chapter and fill in the section on how you respond externally. Below
are some common reactions that may be similar to yours.

❏ I shout at her to stop.

❏ I move quickly over to her and move her a little roughly away
   from what she is doing.

❏ I lecture her quietly while clenching my teeth and holding
   back my anger.

❏ I slap her hand away.

❏ I yell, "No, No, No!"

❏ I cross my arms and give her that "don't you dare" face.

❏ I grab the object.

• • • • • • • • • • • •

The idea is to react as little as possible. We want to show our child
that this action no longer gets them the reaction or attention they are
looking for. Change your reaction in the following ways:

• Do not acknowledge verbally that this matters to you.

• Do not acknowledge physically that this matters to you. For
  example, do not make a facial expression that would denote
  displeasure or shake your head or wag your finger.

• Carry on with whatever you were doing at the time they
  button push. If you are playing a game together, carry on
  with this game. If you were talking to her, carry on with the
  conversation. If you are involved with your own activity, carry
  on with that activity. This way you are showing them that this
  action does not get you to react in the same way anymore.
  Your child will conclude that this is no longer a button to push

inside of you and will stop doing that activity to get you to react.

- Wait a few minutes before you take any action. For example, if their button push was to pee on the floor, wait a few minutes before you clean it up.

- If your child is talking to you about a subject that you previously found challenging, answer their questions or talk about the topic in a calm and understated way.

Special note: To know how to respond to a button push when your child hits you, see chapter 8.

React in a huge way to something you do want them to do

As I have already said, our children are doing this activity to get a reaction from us. So let's give them a reaction to something we *do* want them to do. Find a time when your child is doing something that you want them to continue to do, such as:

- touching you gently

- eating a food item you wanted them to eat

- peeing on the potty

- drawing on the paper and not the wall

- dancing

- singing a song

- looking at you.

Give them a huge reaction when they do anything you want them to do. This is the time to jump up and down, vary your voice in interesting ways, wave your arms in the air, and dance in a funny way. Tell them how wonderful this is. Now your child has something to do to get your reaction, and it just happens to be something you want them to do too!

I will illustrate how to do this using the example of a child I worked with who was peeing on the floor instead of the toilet. I knew this was a button push because while he was peeing he was staring at me, eyes shining, waiting for my response. In a situation like this you would do the following:

1. Relax. Take a deep breath and remember that this is not the end of the world. A little pee on the floor will not hurt anyone and can be cleaned up.

2. Remind yourself that your child is doing this only to get a reaction from you, and that by relaxing you will be closer to helping your child not to do this.

3. Don't externally react to the peeing on the floor. Keep verbally quiet about it. Keep your facial expressions the way they were before you noticed your child pee on the floor. If you were smiling, keep smiling; if you had a relaxed neutral expression, keep that. Carry on with what you were doing. If you were talking to your child about something, carry on with that topic of conversation. If you were in an activity with your child, keep doing that activity. If you were doing a chore, keep on doing that chore.

4. Wait a few minutes before you clean up the pee. When you clean it up do so in a quiet, calm, and understated way.

5. In the next 30 minutes find something that your child is doing that you want to give a really big huge and wonderfully fun reaction to, so that if your child wants to continue to button push, they can do *that* activity instead of peeing on the floor.

EXERCISE 6.4

Now take a moment and think about how you are going to respond differently to your child's button pushing. Go to the button pushing worksheet at the end of the chapter and fill in the last section; this will help you to be fully prepared to respond differently the next time you notice your child button pushing.

BUTTON PUSHING ACTION CHECKLIST

☐ Check to see if your child is button pushing by seeing if they are displaying the following signs:

　☐ They look at you while they are doing the activity.

　☐ They look at you right after they have done the activity.

　☐ They announce to you that they have just done the activity.

　☐ They smile or laugh when you react to what they have just done.

　☐ They do it again right after you have asked them not to while looking at you.

☐ Deactivate the button push.

☐ Internally relax: soften your thoughts surrounding the action your child is doing.

☐ Remind yourself that they are only doing this activity to see your reaction.

☐ Remind yourself that if you do not react they will most likely stop doing the activity.

☐ Do not react verbally.

☐ Do not react physically.

☐ Carry on with what you were doing before your child started the button-pushing activity.

☐ React in a huge, interesting, and lively way to something your child does that you want them to continue to do.

•••••••••••••

Button Pushing Worksheet

1. Write down examples of what your child does as a button push.

   _____

   _____

   _____

   _____

   _____

   _____

   _____

   _____

   _____

   _____

   _____

   _____

2. Write down your internal experience to your child's button push.

   _____

   _____

   _____

   _____

   _____

   _____

   _____

   _____

   _____

   _____

   _____

   _____

3. Write down your external reaction to your child's button push.

_____

_____

_____

_____

_____

_____

_____

_____

_____

_____

_____

4. Now write down the new way you are going to respond to your child's button push, both internally and externally.

_____

_____

_____

_____

_____

_____

_____

_____

_____

_____

_____

Chapter 7

THE TANTRUM RESCUE

Tantrum. Meltdown. Wig-out. Episode. Fit. Whining. Whingeing. Crying. Epi-fit. The big T.

Why are there so many words for one event? Everyone tantrums—it is not just a phenomenon for two-year-olds. Ten-year-olds, 13-year-olds, 18-year-olds, 30- and 40-year-olds, and even my 89-year-old granddad tantrums. Toddlers, teenagers, college students, politicians, celebrities, teachers, police officers—everyone does it. If we think it will get us what we want, we give it a good try. It can be a powerful tool and very effective. The appeal never seems to diminish. We even seem to like watching it on TV. It is modeled so frequently in our society and world that we have to have many names for this one event. One underlying belief that the Western world sells is "I should get everything I want now." This supports and fuels the tantrum phenomenon.

Our children do not use the tantrum because they are on the autism spectrum; they use the tantrum because they are human beings. Our children have tantrums in common with typically developing children, and except for a couple of areas they do it for similar reasons.

WHAT IS THE TANTRUM?

I see all the following behaviors listed below as variations on the tantrum *when they are used in response to our children not getting what they want*:

- the full-blown Grade A rock star performance of yelling, screaming, falling to the ground, and throwing things

- crying

- shouting

- talking with "an attitude," which means they are talking in a "bossy," demanding way; their tone may be a little curt and slightly raised

- pouting and giving you the silent treatment

- hitting the side of their own head repeatedly or biting the side of their hand by the thumb

- head banging

- crying and hitting you

- yelling and knocking things over or throwing things.

When I use the word tantrum in this chapter I am referring to all the behaviors above, and you can use the techniques in this chapter in response to any one of them. Your child may do the actions above for a number of reasons. I would call any one of these behaviors a tantrum when they are used in response to your child not getting what he wants.

WHY DO OUR CHILDREN USE THE TANTRUM IN ALL ITS VARIATIONS?

It works. It is our children's job to find out what will get them what they want in the quickest way. If your child is using the tantrum then it is usually because it gets them the thing that they want quicker than anything else they might have tried. This is the case whatever level of language your child has—verbal, or not verbal yet. I am sure you can all remember a time when you were busy cooking or doing some other important errand for your family. Your special child is either in the kitchen with you or in another room chatting to himself, maybe babbling away, or maybe reciting a scene from a movie. You go about your cooking not paying attention to the language your child is producing, probably glad to be able to get on with your activity. Then suddenly your child starts to scream or cry, your parental antenna goes up, and you rush to his aid. Here the unintentional message you give to your child is, screaming and crying are more useful than speaking to get Mom and Dad's attention.

Another example is when you are doing your weekly shop, your child wants you to open a bag of chocolate chip cookies so that they can start eating them, and you give them two cookies. They want more. Maybe they let you know this by saying "More cookie" or nonverbally by putting the bag in your hand again; you say no, they try again and maybe they even lean in and kiss you. You say no, they start to cry, and then they begin to make a scene; they cry, loudly, the people around you start to stare and so, in order to avoid this public scene, you give them another cookie: anything to stop the staring. Here the unintentional message you are giving your child is: "If I cry I will get what I want." It is more effective than any verbal or nonverbal communication.

A further example is when you and your child are playing together and they are being very interactive with you; how you love this beautiful time together! Then suddenly they stop and they want to watch a video; because you so love the interaction you were just having, you do not want them to—you want to keep playing with them. They are persistent; hand you the DVD, or verbally communicate, "Play DVD." You stick to your guns and say no: they start to cry; you still say no. Then after a few more minutes of crying you start to feel that maybe you are mean not giving them the DVD. You think that you are making them sad and you want them to think that you are a good parent; so you pop the DVD in for them. Again, the unintentional message you give your child is "Crying will get me what I want" and that it is more effective than any verbal or nonverbal communication.

I am sure that most of us will relate to these sentiments and examples! Even if they are not exactly what happens in your daily life with your children, you will have your own similar version.

While helping parents with their children's tantrums, some share with me that they do not experience themselves as giving their children what they want when they tantrum. Maybe as you are reading this you are feeling that way too. *However, in my experience, a child only continues to use the tantrum to get what they want because someone is responding to it.* Maybe you do not respond to the tantrum seven times out of ten, which is a high ratio. However, from your child's point of view, it still means that it works! If you do respond to their tantrum three times out of ten, it is worth using this tantrum method each time, because there is a chance that this is the time they will get what they want. Our children find it hard to express their wants verbally, so it makes good sense for them to use the tantrum, even if it only sometimes works. So really be honest with yourself about your responses to the tantrum. It is not about being right or wrong; it is about understanding yourself and seeing clearly how you are responding to your child so that you can help them. Usually when parents really start to think about all the times their children tantrum they can find examples of when they did respond. You are not alone in this. I myself have had to work through my own feelings about the tantrum. Once I became more comfortable with the tantrum and did not feel the need to stop it, I was then able to help children find a more effective way to communicate. Once we know what we are doing then we can begin to change.

CHANGE OUR THOUGHTS, CHANGE OUR ACTIONS

The way to decrease our children's use of crying and the tantrum is to change the way we respond. It is about showing our children that it does not work anymore. In order to do that it is important for us to identify why we are responding in the first place. Finding the reason helps us adopt a different thought pattern about the tantrum, which will help change our response to it.

The first step is to identify how we are thinking and feeling when our children tantrum. The exercise below will help you do that.

EXERCISE 7.1

Ask yourself, *What thoughts run through my head when my child tantrums?* Write down your first recollections. Or wait until the next time your child tantrums and listen to the thoughts that run through your head. If you are having difficulty, use the list below; just tick the ones that are relevant to you.

- ☐ Oh no, here we go again!
- ☐ I can't go through this again.
- ☐ I have no idea how to handle this.
- ☐ Why me?
- ☐ There has to be something I am doing wrong.
- ☐ I hate autism.
- ☐ I wish I lived elsewhere.

- ☐ Will he always be like this?
- ☐ I am no good at this.
- ☐ What will the neighbors think?
- ☐ I hope the neighbours don't call the police.
- ☐ What will he be like if he does this at 18 years old?
- ☐ I'd rather be at work.
- ☐ I don't think he likes me.

_____

_____

_____

_____

Next question: *How do I feel emotionally when I first hear my child begin to tantrum?* The list below is to help you; just tick the ones that are relevant to you.

- ☐ Sad
- ☐ Annoyed
- ☐ Anxious
- ☐ Numb
- ☐ Helpless
- ☐ Panic
- ☐ Bad
- ☐ Fed up
- ☐ Angry
- ☐ Frustrated
- ☐ Calm
- ☐ Furious

_____

_____

_____

_____

Next question: *How does my body respond when my child tantrums?*

☐   I tense my body.

☐   I start to hold my breath.

☐   My heart begins to race.

☐   I tense my jaw.

☐   I clench my teeth.

☐   I turn around or get up quickly.

☐   I start to sigh.

☐   My heart sinks.

☐   My eyes widen.

☐   My palms start to sweat.

_____

_____

_____

_____

• • • • • • • • • • • •

Now that you have identified some of your responses to your child's tantrum you can see that it can evoke powerful feelings and physical responses. It's no wonder we want to move fast and get our children to stop. Our children pick up on the rich mixture of our physical and emotional reactions and use them to their benefit! It is not a malicious act; it is their job to find the quickest route to getting what they want. They are just being children; all children have a sixth sense about their parents, and, as I've written earlier, our children are particularly sensitive, especially to our attitude.

The next step is to become, as we call it in the Son-Rise Program, a "happy detective," and find out the reasons for your emotional reactions; then you can adopt a different perspective, one that will help you respond differently the next time your child tantrums.

Below are some of the most common reasons why we respond to our children's tantrums. Maybe you relate to all of them, maybe just a few or one in particular. If we are to help our children decrease their use of the tantrum, we must first change ourselves. This is not to say that your child's crying is your fault; we are not in control of our children's actions, but we are in control of how we respond to our children's actions. This is about taking control of the way we think so that we can respond with clarity and purpose when our children tantrum.

"I just want it to stop"

This is what our children are counting on. If they pick this up within us they know that it is worth carrying on. Even if our children have to cry for an hour or more, if they feel that they will get what they want, it will be well worth it. Wouldn't you? If at the end someone was going to give you $1000, would you not be happy to cry? When we want them to stop we are more likely to give in and give them the thing that they are crying for, thus reinforcing their belief that it works.

Our society can put pressure on us to fix a child who is crying. I have often heard statements such as "Where's that child's mother? Why is she not stopping that child from crying?" Or "Will somebody, anybody stop that terrible noise that child is making."

We ourselves just want a peaceful time. However, the more we respond to the tantrum the less times we will have a peaceful time. Helping our children now with their tantrum by being less responsive will help them learn to use another way of communicating.

Next time your child cries, instead of thinking, "I just want it to stop," think: *My role is to help them understand that crying is not an effective way to communicate.*

Practice this new thought to yourself as your child tantrums; it will help you stay the course and implement the techniques listed later in this chapter.

"I feel bad because I do not know why my child is crying"

Why should you know? Crying is incredibly unclear; that's why it is helpful to show our children another way of communicating. Just because you are their parent does not mean that you can translate their crying. It really is ok that you do not know; it does not mean that you are a bad parent. When you do not understand why your child is crying, the most important thing is to feel calm and comfortable. It is ok for your child to not be understood every now and then; they will not die from this. They are loved, well fed, have a good home, and all is well. They will get through this, and a good cry never hurt anyone.

When you are comfortable with not knowing why your child is crying, you will have more of your brainpower available to try and figure out what it is they may be trying to communicate to you.

Next time your child is crying and you do not understand, a helpful thought to think would be: *Even if I do not understand why my child is crying I am still a good parent; staying comfortable with this thought will help me be available and stay calm for my child.*

"I feel sorry for my child; he already has enough challenges with his autism"

There is no doubt that our children have to work harder than neuro-typical children, and that they have a different set of challenges. However, our pity will not serve them; it will not help them move toward overcoming their challenges. Giving in to pity means that we may see our children as less capable, and from that point of view we will tend to give them fewer opportunities to grow. When we do not give them opportunities, how can they show us how capable they actually are? How can they grow? Pity can also cloud our eyes, so when we look at our children we only see their challenges, ignoring their strengths and all the amazing things they can do. I am sure that you can find examples where your child will seek out what they want with a powerful determination, as well as examples where they are happy in their own world, enjoying their isms/stims. When I am teaching groups of parents I will ask them to raise their hands if they see their children as being happy while they are isming/stimming. Each time, most if not all parents will raise their hands indicating yes. Indeed that is also my experience. It seems that we are emotionally suffering more from our children's autism than they themselves.

Next time your child cries, a change in thinking could be: *Thinking my child is weak and to be pitied will not serve them. My child is strong and capable and can deal with not getting what he wants.*

"When my child cries it means that they are unhappy. My job is to help my child be happy all the time"

It seems to make obvious sense that if a child cries it means that they are unhappy. But do we really know? If our child cannot tell us how they feel, who are we to make up how they feel? I can cry for many different reasons: I cry when I feel happy and grateful, I cry when I am sad, I cry from relief, and I like to have a good cry during a sad movie. There are varying medical benefits to crying: it oxygenates the brain and exercises the lungs. Do we know which one our child is doing? I am not saying that I know your child is not unhappy, I am just proposing that until the day comes when our children can express their feelings to us, we don't know.

Most likely our children are crying because it works, to get a response; there is no deep-seated unhappiness around it. You have probably noticed that your child can look very forlorn and grief-stricken while they are crying, and then the moment they get their desired object they instantly smile, happy as a lamb. If they had been truly unhappy, surely it would have taken them longer to get over this powerful emotion? I have watched many a child cry, pleading with their parents to have such and such, and while doing so checking out their facial expressions in the mirror, making sure that their performance is picture perfect.

When we are babies we cry to alert our parents to change our diapers and feed us; it is the only way to communicate our needs, and it is a communication, not an expression of emotions. As we grow older we start to be able to use verbal communication to get what we want, using crying less; but when our verbal or nonverbal communication doesn't work for us, we resort to our old communication of crying. I see adults often respond to a crying toddler with: "Why are you so mad?"; "Why are you so sad?"; "What's making you so unhappy?"; or "Baby, come here, let me make it all better for you." By doing this we start to teach our children that not getting what they want in a moment means that they are unhappy. *We actually make that connection for them.*

As a young child, I remember having an accident in the classroom. As I watched the puddle form on the floor beneath me, my teacher came up to me, put her arm around me, and told me not to worry. She had a very concerned look on her face; she told me numerous times that I had done nothing wrong, that I was not to feel embarrassed or upset about this as it was ok. She used the word embarrassed so many times that I came away from the situation with the distinct feeling that I should feel upset and embarrassed about this. I had actually felt completely fine about the episode, but next time I had an accident, I did feel embarrassed. I had been taught the appropriate emotional reaction from a well-meaning teacher, and I had been taught well.

When my niece was seven years old, she was throwing herself on the floor, crying and yelling while informing her dad she was not going to bed. Her dad, getting more and more frustrated at his daughter's performance, left the room for a moment. I told my niece that her tantrum was not going to work. She stopped, turned toward me, and smiled sweetly, "Oh, it will with Dad, just give me some more time." I love how our children will tell us the truth, and she was right; it took her 20 minutes, but in the end her dad let her stay up another hour.

Now it seems to me that as our children get older something changes; at seven to ten years old they know when they are putting on a performance. Then, as they get a little older, they begin to take on the beliefs that we and our world are selling them and they actually start to believe that it is not ok if they do not get what they want. By the time they are teenagers they may well start to be generally unhappy about things not going their way, and they join the unhappy ranks of our society of adults.

I would say that a large proportion of children using the tantrum are not unhappy, they are just communicating that they want something. But as I am not a mind reader, there is a real possibility that your child may be unhappy at times. So let's discuss that possibility a little. Why is it so bad if your child is unhappy? Why is it not ok for them to feel that way for a while? Our society has brainwashed us into thinking that our job as parents is to make our children happy and give them everything that they want. That if we do not then we are somehow amiss. You cannot save your child from their own feelings of discomfort that they are going to feel as they grow. Think of your job as a parent as helping them know that they cannot necessarily control what the world brings them; *but they can choose how they are going to feel about it.* That way we are helping our children have a strong foundation for how to be when their life gets challenging. We can do this by modeling comfort and happiness when they are not feeling either.

Our children look to us to find out how they should feel about a situation. If they are uncertain they look to us to see if things are ok. For me, I feel anxious when there is turbulence in an airplane. When this happens I look to the people who I feel are in charge and know about turbulence, the cabin crew. I look at their faces and try to determine whether or not they are anxious and unhappy about the situation. If they are, I know that I am in big trouble. If they look calm and are going about their business in the normal way, I feel better taking the lead from them.

Our role as a parent is not to make our children happy in every situation, but to be a supportive guide when helping them to navigate life's challenges. If your child is uncertain and possibly unhappy about you leaving them at school, eating a new food, the prospect of having their hair cut, or their inability to express their needs in a way another person understands, your comfort and happiness is going to be extremely important to them. When they turn to look at you and see that you are feeling comfortable about this situation, you communicate to them that all is well, that the situation is not as bad as they thought it was. You give them something to move toward, thus helping them through a transition that will set them up for all the upcoming transitions they will have to make in life. If you feel uncomfortable and feel the need to save them from this situation, you rob them of the opportunity of learning how to cope, and teach them that "Yes indeed, this is something to be unhappy about."

Two beliefs that will be helpful to think about when your child next cries and tantrums are:

- *"I do not know how my child feels, unless he tells me with his words."*

- *"If my child is unhappy then my comfort and happiness will be a great comfort to him, and will help him move through this situation."*

Changing thoughts that are unhelpful and have become beliefs into new, more helpful thoughts can be understood as our ongoing program of retraining ourselves to develop new beliefs that will support our new approach to our children. These new beliefs will help you consistently implement the techniques below.

TECHNIQUES—WHAT TO DO WHEN OUR CHILDREN TANTRUM

Below are the main techniques to use when your child tantrums:

- **Check your attitude.** This is one of the most important things to do when our children tantrum. If we are uncomfortable, they will know that their crying is working and that it is worthwhile carrying on. Engage one of the new thoughts outlined above that will help you feel more comfortable and easy when your child tantrums. This may take some time to practice and feel real, but just keep reengaging the new thought until it becomes more familiar to you. It may be helpful to write out your new thought and put it up on the wall in your house as a reminder. Maybe on your bathroom mirror or another place you regularly look at.

- **Slow down.** When our children cry we want them to get the message that their crying makes us act really slowly, and we become slightly less intelligent. We always want to respond to them showing them that we care and love them and are interested in them, only we do it at a much slower place—I mean a really, really slow pace. *This changes the dynamic from tantrums work, to tantrums make people slower and don't help me get what I want.* As we move really slowly to their tantrum we want to start moving faster to their verbal and nonverbal communications. We will want to do that at all times, not just around the times when they tantrum. This will give them a very important contrast that will help them understand that if they want something, the fastest way to get it is to use their words or nonverbal communication. We want them to see that the dynamics have changed. We now move very, very slowly when they tantrum, and become very fast and useful when they communicate by using their sounds, words, and nonverbal communication. If we do this, our children will notice! They will shift to the more effective communication.

- **Explain.** Tell them that you don't understand them when they cry. That you want to be helpful; it is just that you do not know what they want. That when they cry and shout it makes it harder for you to know what they are saying. Express this in a calm, relaxed voice, even if your child is yelling or crying loudly.

- **Give reasons.** Tell them why you cannot give them the thing that they are using the tantrum for. Let them know that the food they want is not healthy for them and you want them to feel good in their bodies so that they can be well enough to play. Or that it is the middle of the night and everyone is sleeping and that you want them to sleep so that they are rested for all the fun they will have the next day. Let them know that you do not have enough money to buy a new toy, but when they get home they can play with all the toys they have at home. We want them to know the reasons why we are not giving them something so that they can see that we are caring for and doing our best, not punishing them.

- **Give them another way to communicate.** Let them know what they could do that would help you understand. They could use their words, or show you physically by taking you by the hand and showing you or looking at the thing they want.

- **Give them an alternative.** I would suggest you do this when your child is crying because they want something that either you cannot give them or do not want to give them. For example, if your child wants another cookie, you could offer an apple. If they want a particular stuffed animal that you do not have, you would offer them a different stuffed animal. This way we are still showing our children that we are useful and are trying to be helpful to them. We also model to them that even if they do not get exactly what they want, there are other options that could be fun as well.

- **Be lovingly persistent.** Keep doing all the above. It may take us doing these when our child tantrums a bunch of times before they really get that we have changed the way we respond. Don't forget that you have been responding in a certain way for the whole of your child's life; it may take them a while to realize that you have changed. Keep persisting and showing your child that things have changed and you are no longer responding. When they are convinced you have changed, they will change. The time it takes to convince our children will vary from child to child; all you have to do is keep putting into practice the techniques above.

There are different reasons and circumstances when our children use the tantrum. In each circumstance we would use a different combination of the techniques listed above. The following examples illustrate which combination of techniques to use.

Example: How to respond when my child uses the tantrum to ask for something I do not want to give them

I was working with Maggie, a delightful eight-year-old girl with autism. We were about 45 minutes into the session when she decided she wanted to leave the house. Here is what happened, she goes to the front door and tries to open it. Now, I want us to stay in the house so that we can have a focused session without all the distractions and the obvious dangers of the road and cars. So I knew that I was not going to open the front door and let her out.

I explain to her that we were going to stay inside until our session ended at 5pm. I let her know that she could ask her mom when she returned to go outside, but for now we would be staying inside. I ask her to let me know what she wanted to do outside and that I would try and play it with her inside. Upon hearing this she starts to cry and puts my hand on the doorknob. I first check in with my attitude and choose to feel comfortable and easy about her using the tantrum. I make sure that all my movements are *slow*, so that she can see that her tantrum does not make me move fast but actually makes my actions slower and me a little confused.

As she cries I explain, "I will not open the door even if you cry. It is important that we stay inside so that we can play together and not have to be distracted by all the cars, people, and things outside. Maybe your mom will take you out later at 5pm." She then cries even louder and throws herself on the floor, kicking her legs and thrusting her arms around. As she does this she looks straight at me, watching to see what I will do. In response I say to her: "Even if you throw yourself on the floor and scream we are not going outside." As I say these things to her I am feeling very loving and kind toward her; I am smiling and talking in a calm, loving voice.

She looks at me and then picks up the stool and starts to throw it at me; I catch it easily and say to her: "Even if you throw things, the door will stay closed and we will not be playing outside."

After I say this, Maggie, still crying, goes into the bathroom and turns on all the taps, rustles the shower curtain, knocks over the garbage can, and throws the toilet paper into the toilet. She then comes out and looks at me. I say to her: "Even if you knock things over and make a mess the door will remain closed and we will stay inside."

She leaves her biggest card to last, she takes off all her clothes, bangs her chest, and looks at me defiantly with her hands on her hips, as if to say, "Now what are you going to do?" Again I say to her: "Even if you take off all your clothes the door will remain closed and we will be staying inside."

After this explanation she stops crying and with my help puts her clothes back on. None of her usual tricks had worked on me, so she went back to playing. It did not take her any time to transition from her tantrum to playing. Once she realized that I was not moved by her tantrum she completely stopped, and played with me as she had done so before. Wasn't Maggie so clever in what she chose to do to try and get me to open the door? I often marvel at our children's intelligence and understanding of how to motivate the people around them. That's why it is so important that we change how we react, instead of focusing on changing our child's reaction.

It may take your child some time to really believe that you will no longer respond to their tantrums, that their tantrum will not change the situation, but if you can be lovingly persistent with this approach they *will* eventually get it. By changing in this way you will also be teaching them something else: *Sometimes you do not get what you want, and that is ok.*

Your child could use the tantrum to try and get a number of different things you either do not have or do not want to give them. It could be anything, such as:

- a food you do not want them to eat

- a toy that you do not want to buy for them

- a toy that you cannot find

- a walk outside, but it is raining

- a drive in the car when it is bedtime

- a trip to McDonald's or another store when you do not want to go

- a DVD at 12 o'clock at night.

EXERCISE 7.2

On the lines provided below write down what it is that your child uses the tantrum for that you either cannot or do not want to give them.

_____

_____

_____

_____

_____

_____

_____

_____

_____

_____

_____

_____

_____

In these circumstances engage the techniques listed earlier in this chapter.

1. **Check your attitude.** Adopt a belief that is useful for you not to give in to the tantrum, such as "I know that the thing they want is not useful for them; I am not letting them have it because I am the parent and can see the whole picture and

am helping them by not giving it to them" and/or "It is ok for my child to not get what they want; it is a useful skill to teach them that they can be happy even if they do not get what they want."

2. **Slow down.** Lower your energy and talk and move slowly. Remember that when I say slowly I mean really, really slowly. We want to show our children that things take longer when they tantrum.

3. **Explain.** Tell them that even if they tantrum it will not help them get what they want.

4. **Give reasons.** Tell them the reasons why this is. If they want something in the middle of the night, let them know that everyone is asleep and we do not want to wake anyone up and it is the time for them to sleep. Or that you are not giving them the food that they want because it is not healthy for them and you want them to be healthy and strong so that they can do all the things that they love to do.

5. **Give them an alternative.** If they wanted a food item that was not healthy for them you could offer them a healthy item. If they wanted to go to McDonald's you could write out the McDonald's logo. If they want a certain book that you do not have you could offer them a different book. This shows our children that even if we cannot or do not want to give them the exact thing they are asking for we are still trying to be helpful to them.

6. **Be lovingly persistent.** You have a history with your child; they are used to you responding to their tantrum, so it may take time for your child to believe that you have changed. They will most likely think, "Oh, I just have to keep crying and eventually Mom will give me what I want." So you might find that for a while they will start to escalate their tantrum behavior as if to say, "Ok, so you are not responding to my crying, but how about my hitting?" or "How about if I scream louder, or longer?"

Once you have done all the techniques above and your child is still crying, then I would suggest that you let your child know that it is ok with you if they continue to cry, as you know it won't get them what they want; you are going to do something else, but they are welcome to stay where they are and keep crying if they so choose. Then go to a different part of the room, or a different part of the house. You could start doing a household chore or play something by yourself that you know your child likes. The important thing is that you take your energy off your child, thus letting them know that their tantrum is not working on you. Remember, it is not about getting your child to stop, but about communicating to your child that you have moved on. You are communicating to your child that their tantrum no longer has currency with you. You are also giving them the opportunity to experience letting go of something they want—a valuable life lesson.

Example: How to respond when my child uses the tantrum and I do not know why

I have often been in situations where I am working with a child who cries for long periods of time either non-stop or off and on, and I really do not have any idea why they are crying. The example below is of a little three-year-old named Frank, who would cry on and off for most of the day. It shows how I used the techniques I have already outlined in this chapter to help him, as well as another technique that is useful when we really do not know why our children are using the tantrum.

1. **I checked my attitude.** The beliefs I engaged with were: "This is not about stopping Frank crying—it is about helping him find another way to communicate what is going on for him" and "Frank's crying means nothing about me."

2. **I slowed down.** The whole time I was with him I moved at a slow and methodical pace, never rushing or moving fast— thus showing that crying did not make me move fast.

3. **I explained.** I told him that I did not understand him when he cried, but I really did want to help him.

4. **I gave an alternative.** I told him what he could do to help me know what he wanted. That he could use his words, or take me to the place where the thing he may want is, or look at it with his eyes.

5. **I tried to be useful.** When he did not let me know what he wanted in a different way I slowly, and I mean really slowly, began to offer him things. When we move slowly we send the message that people don't understand the tantrum, a very important message for our children to get! First I offered him food, as maybe he was hungry; then I offered him a drink; and then I checked to see if he needed a diaper change. When none of these were the case, I checked to see that all was well with his body. Maybe he had hurt himself and could not tell me. Maybe there was something in the environment that was bothering him. I dimmed the lights and shut off the fan; I offered him a cold washcloth and the hot washcloth; In the end I got lucky and he stopped crying when I gave him a hot washcloth, he took it and started to chew on it. It took me 45 minutes of slowly offering things to find out what he wanted. I then let him know that if he had taken me to where the washcloth was or said the word, I could have got it for him a lot quicker.

With the example of Frank, as with all our children who tantrum, it is important to be lovingly persistent and to keep employing the techniques above. Keep slowly offering things as a way to be useful. Once you feel that you have offered as many things as you can think of and your child has declined all of them and keeps pushing you away while they cry, then I suggest you tell them that you have tried everything you know to be useful to them, and that you still do not understand their crying, so you are going to do something else. Tell them that you are still here to help them and that they can come and let you know what they need by telling you or showing you whenever they want and you will be only too glad to help them. Then, as in the previous example, take your energy off your child by moving away. Go to a different part of the room, or a different part of the house. Quietly begin to do a household chore or quietly play something by yourself that you know your child likes. The important thing is that you take your energy off your child as this may help them work through what is happening for them. Then come back ten minutes later and again start using the techniques I have outlined.

Consistency is the key. Share these concepts and techniques with all your family members. It's like the TV quiz show *The Weakest Link.*

For our child to believe that the tantrum does not work anymore we have to make sure that there are no weak links in our children's life. It is important that you and your partner are on the same page. If your child's grandparents, aunts, and uncles are regularly involved in your child's life, then pass this information on to them. You will most likely be able to tell who is not following your new protocol to the tantrum as your child will most likely stop using the tantrum with everyone but this person. So have a chat with that person; see which stage they are having the most difficulty with and help them out a little.

NOT ALL CRYING IS A TANTRUM
When our children cry out of physical distress

Sometimes our children cry because they are feeling unwell or have just had a minor accident like falling over and stubbing their toe. Obviously, if this is the reason, we want to be as effective as we can in helping them have more physical ease. Often there will be other signs that help you know that this is the case. For instance, they may hold their head, or rub the part of the body that hurts, and want to lie down for most of the day. Maybe you just witnessed them fall over and bang their head or scrape their knee. If your child is a picky eater, maybe eating only two food types, or has chronic constipation or diarrhea, the chances are that he is having digestive challenges (see chapter 12) and may cry when he is in physical distress. If this is the case they may start to cry just before they poop or afterwards, or after they have eaten or drunk something.

Your comfort and ease are important to apply here as well. When you are comfortable even with the physical distress of your child, you have more of your brainpower available to you to be helpful and present with what is going on for your child. It does not mean that you are cold or indifferent to any suffering your child might be feeling. When you panic or become uncomfortable, it becomes more about you and less about your child. At a time like this your child needs your loving attention; it is hard to be loving when you are unhappy. When you are comfortable, you will be more creative and find more ways to help your child. I know for myself when I am unwell I prefer to be around a happy person and will move away from people who think what is happening to me is terrible. *My pity does not help my child.*

Physical distress is physical only. In our society we often mistake physical distress for mental distress or some form of unhappiness. It is not always the case, especially for children. When children are sick they can still engage in play and the things that interest them. It does not stop them laughing at a funny joke or enjoying a good story. In fact, laughter has been proven to be good medicine (Dunbar *et al.* 2012). So don't assume that just because they do not feel well that that means that they are unhappy.

Some beliefs to engage when your child is physically distressed are: "My child may be in physical distress but that does not necessarily mean that he is unhappy" and "My comfort in this situation will be the best way to take care of and help my child."

Techniques

1. **Check your attitude** and engage one of the useful attitudinal beliefs listed above.

2. **Slow down**—have an energy that is not too loud or too fast for your child.

3. **Explain** to them what is going on with their bodies and how you are going to help them. Tell them that it is ok if they want to cry, but maybe rubbing their knee or the part of the body that hurts, and taking any medication you want to give them, will help them more than crying.

4. **Give them another way to communicate** to you that they feel unwell. You could tell them that the word for this is "sick" or "hurt"; use this word as you rub their tummy or bandage their knee, so that they can associate this word with feeling unwell.

5. **Be useful**—offer different things like massages, stomach rubs for stomachaches, or head rubs for headaches; give any medication that you feel will be helpful. All the time you are doing any of the above explain that you are doing these things to help them feel better.

6. **Give them an alternative**—once you have done the above give your child something else to focus their attention on.

For instance, read them their favorite book, play their favorite song on the CD player, or draw them pictures you know they will like. Or write the alphabet or any pattern you know your child uses to soothe themselves.

Crying that appears suddenly without apparent cause

Many parents share with me that their children will cry suddenly "out of the blue" and that they cannot see any circumstances as to what may have caused their crying.

Stress levels

Your child may just be over-stimulated and/or too tired. Think about their day. Have they been to many outside places, perhaps school and then on to therapy, swimming, a trip to the mall, etc.? Is the house full of your relatives or friends speaking loudly? Sometimes our children will suddenly start crying because they have reached their limit with their stress levels. Crying is an expression of this overload and can be an outlet of the stress building up in their bodies. If you consider this to be the case, then take them to a quieter room in the house, a place with fewer outside stimulants where they can regain some sense of control over their environment again.

Inflexibility

Our children have autism, and a common trait amongst children with autism is that they can be inflexible and need some patterns, routines, and rituals to remain the same. When she was younger, my godchild Jade had a bedtime routine that needed to be executed in a particular order. When I was babysitting her, if I was to get the order wrong, for instance turn down her bed covers before I had moved her teddy bears, she would begin to cry and there was really nothing I could do to soothe her. I always did my best to carry out the routine in the way I knew she wanted it. This was my way of showing her that I loved her, that I was user-friendly, and that I could be trusted to give her control. But sometimes her routine changed without me knowing. In this case I would do the following:

- Check my attitude—engage a useful belief: "Sometimes I will break the order my child wants because I did not know and that is ok."

- Move slowly.

- Explain to her that there must have been something that I did out of order but that I did not do that on purpose, that if she could tell me what it is instead of crying then I will know better for next time.

- I would suggest that you do a home-based therapy to help your child with their flexibility (like the Son-Rise Program). Here is a link to techniques that will help your child be more flexible: www.autismtreatmentcenter.org/contents/other_ sections/aspergers-autism-treatment.php.

Yes/no contrary pattern

This is a term I have coined for when nothing seems to satisfy our children. When given exactly what they ask for they suddenly want the opposite! For example, I was working with Mikey, a six-year-old mid-verbal child with autism. He brought me his sock and said "Sock on." I praised him for bringing the sock to me and asking so wonderfully to put the sock on, and I immediately put his sock on. As soon as the sock was on he asked me to take it off, which I did. We did this a number of times and then he started to cry at the same time as telling me to take his sock off and on. This carried on for another 25 minutes before he stopped asking me and kept his sock on. I have worked with numerous other children who do some version of this yes/no contrary pattern.

We could spend a lot of time theorizing about what he really wanted. Maybe there was a particular way he wanted me to put his sock on that I was not doing. Maybe he really wanted me to scratch his foot but did not have the vocabulary for it. Both of these could be true. I do feel though that, whatever the reason, it comes under the category of our children needing some sort of control over their environment. It is an expression of their inflexibility, which is an expression of their autism, not a tantrum. In this situation I would suggest that you give control and do what your child is asking until they work through this contrariness. In doing so, we show that we are user-friendly, someone who is useful to talk to and go to when they are feeling this way. The more our children come to us, the more opportunities we have to help them with their inflexibility.

TANTRUM ACTION CHECKLIST

☐ Check your comfort level when your child tantrums.

☐ Adopt one of the following beliefs to help you feel more comfortable:

    ☐ My job is not to stop my child from using the tantrum, it is to show them that it is not an effective way to communicate.

    ☐ It is ok if I do not understand why my child is crying. I am still a good parent. My comfort will help me help my child.

    ☐ My role as a parent is not to make my child happy in every situation, but to be a guide, helping them through life's challenges.

☐ Slow down and move slowly when your child tantrums.

☐ Explain to your child that you do not understand their crying. It does not help you know what they want.

☐ Show and ask them to communicate in another way:

    ☐ Use their words.

    ☐ Use their sounds.

    ☐ Look at the object they want.

    ☐ Let them take you by the hand and show you what they want.

☐ Consider the following if they are using the tantrum to get something you do not want to give them:

    ☐ Offer them an alternative.

    ☐ Explain to them that even their tantrum will not help them get what they want.

- ❏ Be consistent using these techniques each time your child tantrums.

- ❏ Create consistency—teach these techniques to all the people who care for your child.

- ❏ Consider that not all crying is a tantrum.

  - ❏ Use the following techniques if your child is in physical distress:

    - ❏ Check your attitude.

    - ❏ Explain what is happening with their bodies.

    - ❏ Give them another way to communicate what hurts.

    - ❏ Be helpful.

    - ❏ Give an alternative focus.

  - ❏ Take them to a quieter place in your house if they are over-stimulated.

  - ❏ Give them control and be user-friendly by responding to their "Nos" and "Yeses" if they are inflexible or in a yes/no contrary pattern.

A mom recently told me a story about her son Dillon, who is now seven and after doing a home-based Son-Rise Program for two and a half years is in full-time school without an aide. His teacher just told her that when a boy was crying at his school he went up to his teacher and said to her, "I don't think he knows that crying is not a useful way to get what he wants." Dillon had been listening to his mom. What a powerful tool his mom had taught Dillon, one that will serve him for the rest of his life.

Chapter 8

HITTING AND INTENSE ENERGY

This chapter is about how to help our children when they hit, bite, scratch, pinch, kick, slap, punch, or pull the hair of another person, or use any type of physical force. In my 25 years of working with children and adults, I have been hit, strangled, kicked, punched, pinched, bitten, slapped, head butted, and scratched by little children, as well as by adults who were far taller and heavier than me. I have been with a child who continually tried to hit, bite, and scratch me for over an hour. I have been with an adult who was much heavier and stronger than me, where I was not sure that I would be able to physically look after myself. If you are in any of these situations and you do not know what to do or how to handle it, know that I have been there too, and through the Son-Rise Program I learned attitudes and strategies that are highly effective in helping our children learn to manage their intense energy and to be gentle with others. It is these techniques that I outline in this chapter. They are time tested and have been effective with numerous children on the spectrum.

Just the other day I was talking to the great mom of Ariel, a lovely five-year-old with autism. When I first met this mom her arms were literally black and blue from bruises. Ariel had periods every day where she would pinch and bite her mom's arms, face, and legs. Her mom completely changed her attitudinal perspective about why her daughter hit her and put the techniques below into practice. Today Ariel has not pinched or bitten her mom in over six months. Her mom proudly sports a T-shirt exposing her bruise-free arms.

REFRAME WHY YOU THINK YOUR CHILD HITS

The first place to start is to reframe the way we think about why our children might hit. Most parents and professionals describe children as being aggressive or violent when they do the above-mentioned behaviors. In the dictionary *aggressive* is defined as: "Characterized by or tending toward unprovoked offensives, attacks, invasions, or the like; militantly forward or menacing"; *violent* is defined in the dictionary as: "Using extremely forceful actions that are intended to hurt people or are likely to cause damage."

I completely understand how it may feel as if our children are out to attack us and want to hurt us when they hit us. It seems to make sense since it often does hurt! I used to think the same thing. However, it is not our children's intention or the purpose behind why they hit or use physical force. They have other reasons for doing this that may not be apparent to you at first glance. Remember earlier I shared that our children do things for a reason; if we come from this perspective, we can become a detective and look for the signs that our children give us before they hit us that will help us know their reason. The four major reasons our children hit us are the following:

- *They are trying to communicate* something through their hitting. Some of our children have discovered that when they hit people, the people around them move faster and get them what they want more quickly.

- *They want to see our reaction* to their hitting. They want to see us cry, yell, protest, and tell them off.

- *They have sensory challenges* where hitting, biting, and pinching is actually helping them regulate their sensory system.

- *They are trying to protect themselves.* For some of our children they may feel that this is the only way to get some of the people in their lives to stop and listen to them.

All four reasons are very different from wanting to hurt us or attack us, although of course it is totally understandable why you may have thought otherwise. That is why in the Son-Rise Program we do not label this behavior as "aggressive" or "violent"—we call it "intense energy." The label "intense energy" has none of the judgmental associations that the word "aggressive" or "violent" has, and more accurately describes what is happening. So from this point forward I will refer to all hitting, biting, pinching, and physical force as "intense energy."

It may seem as if your child very suddenly "out of the blue" hits you or someone else for no reason that you can see. Indeed, when I first started to work with children on the autism spectrum, I believed this too. My training has taught me how to really observe a child and notice what is going on in their environment, their physical bodies, and the relationship between what I did and what they did. Once I could do this it became very apparent that not only were there clear reasons why our children have intense energy, but also that they give very clear signs beforehand. The great news about this is that once you know the signs you will see them and you will never have to get hit, scratched, kicked, or bitten by your child again. You will see it coming and be able to get out of the way.

Learning to observe and notice the signs is crucial, not only so that you can get out of the way, but because they are also clues to the reason your child hits you. Once you know the reasons then you can apply the specific strategies that will help your child stop hitting and using physical force. Each reason will have a different set of strategies to apply.

Below are 4 checklists that group the most common signs/and actions our children do either before or during times of intense energy. Read all four checklists and check off the signs/actions that are relevant for your child.

Checklists

Checklist 1: Communication

Check off any of the actions below if you see your child doing them around the time they had intense energy.

- ☐ They pinch/hit/bite/punch right after you have told them that they cannot have something.

- ☐ They have had trouble making their needs understood. Maybe they have been physically moving you around trying to get you to do something. You were trying to help them but you had no idea what they wanted.

❏ They hit you during a game. It could have been a rough-and-tumble game or a chase or tickle game. Maybe it was even during a singing game or a board game.

Checklist 2: Seeing your reactions

Check off any of the actions below if you see your child doing them around the time they had intense energy.

❏ They look at you directly in the eye while they hit you, or directly after.

❏ They smile, laugh, or flap their hands excitedly as you react to their hitting you.

❏ They chase you to try and hit you again.

❏ They seem happy and content with the consequence you gave them.

Checklist 3: Sensory challenges

Check off any of the actions below if you see your child doing them around the time they had intense energy.

❏ They were jumping up and down intensely.

❏ They tensed part of their bodies, for example tensing their face so much that it may shake a little. They might clench their jaw as they do this.

❏ They banged a part of their body vigorously with either their own hand or an object.

❏ They ran around the house or room with increased energy.

❏ They yelled sounds louder and longer than usual.

❏ They became more intense and faster in reciting their scripts from movies or books.

❏ They urgently fired questions at you when you know they know the answer.

☐ They got into a contrary pattern, where they ask for something, then say no when you give it to them, then ask for it again, then say no when you re-offer it, and so forth.

Checklist 4: Protecting themselves

Check off any of the actions below if you see your child doing them around the time they had intense energy.

☐ They stopped your attempts to interact with them. For example, you may pick up a toy and play with it and they take it out of your hands.

☐ They said or indicated "No" to your play suggestions. For example, you may have sung and they said "No" or put their hand over your mouth. This may have happened three or four or more times in a row.

☐ They moved away from your attempts to touch them or be physically close to them.

Look at which checklist has the most checked off. Then use the techniques and strategies that correspond to that checklist. If it is Checklist 1, read the section below called "When your child is using intense energy as a way to communicate their wants." If it is Checklist 2, read the section called "When your child is using intense energy to see your reaction." If it is Checklist 3, read the section called "When your child is using intense energy as a way to take care of their sensory challenges." And if it is Checklist 4, read the section called "When your child is using intense energy as a way to protect themselves."

Special note: You may find that your child has two checklists of signs— that is not unusual. We can all do things for different reasons. Let's take eating: sometimes I eat because I am hungry; other times I eat because I want to taste the sweetness of food, like chocolate; or other times I may eat because I am sad. Our children can use intense energy for different reasons too. For example, you may find on one occasion that your child displays the signs in Checklist 1, so on that occasion apply those strategies; but on another day she displays signs in Checklist 2, so on that occasion you would apply those strategies.

Stategies
When your child is using intense energy as a way to communicate their wants

You are reading this because your child's signs were mainly in Checklist 1. If this is the case your child is most likely using intense energy as a form of communication. They are hitting, biting, slapping, pinching, or head banging to let you know that they want something.

Here are three examples. In the first example, Tommy and his mom are at the toy store. Tommy wanted to buy another Thomas the Tank Engine train; he asked his mom, "I want train." Knowing that he already had ten at home, his mom said, "No, you have some at home." Tommy persisted, saying, "Yes, want train." His mom said again, "No, you have enough trains." Then Tommy hit his mom's arm, to which his mom said, "Ok then," and bought the train. Tommy's mom bought him the train because she wanted to avoid a "scene" in the shop; the unintentional message she gave Tommy was that hitting is a useful way not only to express what you want, but to get what you want.

In the second example, I was watching Greg and his dad play together. They were having a wonderful time wrestling with one another. Greg's dad stopped playing for a bit and told his son he was tired. Greg then hit his dad on the head. His dad thought this was Greg's way to initiate the game again, so he started wrestling with Greg once more, saying, "Does that mean you want to play more?"— again unintentionally giving Greg the message that hitting is a way to initiate play.

In the third example, Mary is in the kitchen with her mom. She was pulling her mom by the arm indicating that she wanted something. Her mom had no idea what she wanted. Mary was yet to be verbal, so it was understandable that her mom did not know what she wanted. Her mom was trying to be useful, and after a moment she said to her daughter, "I don't know what you want, honey," and went to sit down. Mary came to her mom and started to pinch her, to which her mom said, "Ok, Ok, Ok." Thinking that Mary's pinching was a sign of distress, she got up and started in an urgent way to offer her things. Eventually she found out that Mary wanted some ice cubes. Here the unintentional message was I will try harder and faster for you when you pinch me.

Often when children use intense energy the adults around them will move faster and try to "understand" more. Parents tell me that they move faster and give their children the things that they want so that their child will stop hitting them and to avoid a "meltdown." I can see why you would want that; however, the opposite happens. It actually teaches our children to hit more. Our child may begin to think: "Ok, so the way to get more of what I want is to hit, as everyone tries to understand me more and gets me what I want faster." For our children who find communicating challenging you can understand them making this connection and using it. Not in a naughty or manipulative way, but simply as a form of communication.

If this is the case for your child, below are some strategies you can use to help your child learn to communicate in a different way.

- **Think the following thoughts:**

  o   My child is clever! She is trying to get what she wants by the quickest route possible.

  o   She is not trying to hurt me.

- **Move slowly and explain that you do not understand hitting.** This is very important. Right now our children have the message that when they use intense energy the people around them move fast. Thus hitting is a useful thing for them. If we reversed that and gave them the message that it actually makes people respond really slowly, then it would not be useful for them to use. This means that when your child hits you, you don't move quickly to try and understand what they want. In fact I would suggest that you tell them in a slow and calm way that you do not understand what their hitting means, directly teaching them that hitting is not a communication that you understand. We want to show our children that any form of intense energy will not help them get what they want anymore. In fact it makes people move slower and they even become slightly confused.

  For example, if this strategy was used in the example of Tommy wanting the train in the shop, when he hit his mom, she could have said, "Tommy, I do not understand what you mean when you hit me," and put the train back on the shelf. Then she would have stood up and looked very confused.

In the example of Greg hitting his father to get him to play the game again, Greg's dad would have said, "I do not understand what you mean when you hit." He would have stayed resting for a while, instead of immediately jumping into action when his son hit him.

In the example of Mary pinching her mom, Mary's mom would have said, "Mary, I do not understand what you mean when you hit me." She would have stayed sitting instead of jumping up and trying to find out what Mary wanted.

- **Make hitting completely ineffective.** This is very important! You want to help your child understand that intense energy of any kind will not get them what they want. In the example we have talked about with Tommy hitting so that his mom would buy him a train, it is really important that we do not buy that train. Even if you were going to buy the train, don't. Not buying it sends the message that hitting is not an effective way to get what you want. This is a very important skill to teach your child, one that will serve them socially in the years to come.

- **Move out of the way.** Now you know that your child hits as a way to get what they want. If they want something to which the answer is "No," do the following:

  o   Know that she may hit you.

  o   Step out of the way, so she cannot reach you with her hands. If your child is small, stand up so they can't hit your face or pull your hair.

  o   If your child is an adult or bigger than you, always have a big therapy ball or a big cushion available that you can put between you and your child to protect yourself. For example, I was working with a 13-year-old boy who would use intense energy when we told him that he could not have something he wanted. We had a big therapy ball. When he asked for something that I knew I did not have or could not provide for him, I would slowly and calmly walk over and get behind the therapy ball before I explained why I could not get it for him. That way, if he decided to hit me, I could put the ball in front of me so that he could not reach me, but hit the ball instead.

- **Offer an alternative.** Once you have moved out of the way, and explained why you cannot give your child what they wanted, offer an alternative. For example, if they wanted a cookie, offer a food you do want to give them. If they wanted the yellow car, offer them a different car or toy. If they want to go outside, you could draw them a picture of the outside instead, and let them know what time they could or will be going outside. This way we are communicating to them that hitting will not get them what they want, *and* that we are trying to be useful to them.

- **Move fast to other forms of communication.** This is so, so important. While we respond slowly to our children's hitting, we want to respond fast to a form of communication that we *want* them to continue to use. So we are highlighting a form of communication that *does* make us move fast and *does* help them get what they want. If we do this for what we want at the same time as responding slowly to hitting and letting them know we don't understand that, they will start to use the other form of communication.

So let's make a conscious decision to respond quickly and fast to all our children's verbal and nonverbal communication when they take you by the hand, point, make sounds, or talk to you. You may think, "Well of course I do that already." However, if our children are hitting to communicate their wants, it means that we are not responding fast enough to their other forms of communication. This can be understandable as you often have a lot to do. You have household chores, job responsibilities, your other children, phone calls, texts, emails, etc. There is often so much going on that their communications can at times go unnoticed. This, however, is something we can easily change by having the intention to focus on their other forms of communication more.

This means that next time you are on the phone and your child comes over to you and starts talking to you, respond straight away to their verbal communication. If you and your husband are talking in the kitchen and your child comes in and asks for something, respond straight away to that request, showing your child that their verbal communication is the quicker way to get what they want.

For those of you who have children who are yet to be verbal, maybe they have a few words or sounds that they make. That is ok. Make an intention to respond with an action as much as you can to the sounds that your child is making. You can do this even if you do not understand what your child wants. For example, when your child says a sound, maybe an "eee" sound, do the following:

○   Jump up and say, "That was a great sound."

○   Put an action to the sound and make it into a word; you could get them some food; or a toy, or sing them a song.

○   Once you do that you could say, "I got you that because you made the 'eee' sound," highlighting why you responded in that way.

If your child indicates needs or wants through moving you by the hand or arm, be super-responsive to this, moving wherever your child is pulling you. As soon as they move you, move with them and praise them for letting you know what they wanted by moving you in this way. This lets them know that this is a great way to communicate with you and more effective than hitting. If you do these two techniques with your yet-to-be-verbal child it will show her another way to successfully communicate what she wants.

- **Celebrate when your children are gentle.** When our children are being gentle with us, let's praise them. Tell them specifically how we love their gentle touch. You could say something like: "I love that you are holding my hand so nicely" or "Thank you for that lovely gentle hug." Let our children know that we really enjoy it when they interact with us in a gentle way. There are most likely so many times during the day when our children do interact with us in a gentle way; let's highlight these to our children by joyfully celebrating them. Through our celebration we are showing our children that being gentle is the way to interact with people.

- **Be persistent and consistent.** You may already have a history of moving fast when your child hits you, so it may take a little time for your child to realize that this is no longer the way you are going to respond. Keep responding in the way outlined above until they understand this concept. As you do this, know that I am rooting for you—you can do this! Your child is clever, and once it is no longer effective in their lives they will stop. Each time you show your child that her hitting is not an effective way to communicate, know that you are one step closer to your child changing this.

When your child is using intense energy to see your reaction

You are reading this because your child's signs were primarily in Checklist 2, which means that your child is most likely hitting you as a button push. As we talked about in chapter 6, they are hitting you just to see your reaction. They want to hear you say that you "hurt them" or watch your face turn red or you raise your voice. They are interested in your reaction to their hitting, not the hitting itself.

For example, I was working with a ten-year-old boy with high-functioning autism who loved to watch people's reactions to things. He picked up a play hammer and lifted it up over my head, and put on a very intense and grave expression on his face as if he was going to hit me very hard. I already knew that he was doing this so that he could watch my reaction, as I had had a lot of experience with him and knew that he did such things as a button push. So I completely relaxed my body, did not flinch or move away from him, and kept on smiling. When he did not get the reaction he wanted he just said, "Oh," and put the hammer down.

In another example, I was working with an 18-year-old young man with Asperger's, who, after slapping my face, was somewhat mystified when I did not yell at him or lecture him, but had a very calm response to him hitting me. He looked intently into my eyes and said, "But I just slapped you. Should you not be calling someone to come and help you with me?" I replied that I was hoping we could carry on looking at his Pokémon cards. He stared at me a little longer, shrugged his shoulders, and we carried on looking at his cards together. He never slapped me again. This young man was used to people giving him a big reaction and having people come hold him down and put him in timeout at school. He thought it would be the same with me. When he saw that it was different, that I was not going to react in the same way, he had no reason to hit me again.

Our children may hit/pinch/spit to get a reaction from the adults around them, because this is a time when the adults get lively and interesting and pay attention. For instance, when our children are playing quietly in the living room either by themselves or with their siblings, we may be in the same room as them reading the newspaper or doing something else, paying no attention. But when someone gets hit/pinched, etc., we start to pay a lot of attention to the person who is doing the hitting. We may do one of the following:

- Raise our voices and shout and yell.

- Talk in a high-pitched squeaky voice.

- Put on grave, interesting facile expressions.

- Wave our arms and hands around.

- Wag a finger in front of our face.

- Turn bright red in anger and frustration.

Suddenly things have got a lot more interesting!

If your child is using intense energy to see your "interesting" reaction, apply the strategies below:

- **Change your reaction.** Change it to a non-reaction, as if your child had never hit you.

  ○ If you were smiling at the time they hit you, keep smiling.

  ○ If you had a straight face, keep that straight face.

  ○ If you were cooking or doing another household chore, keep on with that activity.

  This is one rare time when I suggest that you do not go into a long explanation about how it is good to be gentle, etc. It is my experience that if your child is using intense energy for this reason, it is the long explanation that they want. Instead, tell them just once as loving and as calmly as you can, "I would love it if you were gentle with me" or "If you are trying to tell me something, I can't really understand what it is from you hitting/biting/kicking me." Then carry on with what you were doing. This way we acknowledge what just happened and what we want without making it the "major event" they are looking for.

- **Give big and fun reactions to your child when they are being gentle.** We know our children are using intense energy to get a reaction from us. So now let's give them a big reaction when they are being gentle with us. The more we react to their loving, gentle interaction, the more they will do this instead of hitting us.

  When your child is being gentle, holding your hand or hugging you, give big and fun reactions. I don't mean just say thank you for being gentle. That is nice, but add a little spice to it so that when your child wants to get your attention and see you react in a fun way they may just touch you gently instead of hitting you. You could:

  ○ sing while you are praising them

  ○ wave your arms in the air as you praise them

  ○ jump up and down as you praise them

  ○ praise them using a funny character voice

  ○ turn into an animal

  ○ use big, animated expressions.

  The idea is to give your child a big reaction for the behavior you want them to do more of. The bigger, the funnier, the better!

When your child is using intense energy as a way to take care of their sensory challenges

You are reading this because your child's signs were primarily in Checklist 3, which means your child's intense energy is most likely focused on them trying to regulate their sensory systems. We know that our children's sensory systems can be very challenged. They may have energy that is building up inside them that they do not know how to successfully release. Children with autism create unique and interesting ways to relieve the build-up of energy and regulate their sensory systems. You may see them bang certain parts of their body, or seek pressure on their feet and hands by jumping up and down or banging their hands on the floor or table. Often a child will dig their chin strongly into my shoulder or hands. These and others are all actions our children take to try and take care of their sensory system. Also the action of biting, squeezing, or pinching actually allows them to release this energy, helping them organize themselves physically.

EXERCISE 8.1

This exercise is for you to experience how squeezing, biting, and pinching can release pressure building up in the body.

- Clasp your hands together and really squeeze them, again not half-heartedly but with all your might.
  - Do this three times, each time lasting at least 20 seconds.
  - Take a moment to reflect on how that felt. Did it release tension in your body? Did it give a strong sensation to your hands?
- Hold a cushion from your couch and hug it close to you as hard as you can for 30 seconds.
  - How did that feel?
- Find an object like a bouncy ball or a washcloth soaked in water.
  - Really bite into it. Yes, I do mean that. Sink your teeth into it with all your might.
  - Do this three times, each time lasting at least 20 seconds.
  - Now reflect on how that felt. How does your jaw feel now—was it a strong sensation? Did it release pressure on your jaw?

What I feel when doing this exercise and what people report is a release of any built-up tension. It feels good to do this! And it is helpful for the body. Our children are doing this for the same reasons.

However, their need to release energy from their bodies is far greater than ours. Our children are just using our bodies as a way to help themselves. The trick here is to help our child use something other than another person to release their energies. If your child is using intense energy for this reason, use the strategies outlined below:

- **Think the following thoughts:**

  - My child is hitting me in an attempt to take care of their sensory system.

  - Their actions are not connected to their love of me, or their respect toward me.

  - I can help my child by giving them more sensory input to help them balance their bodies.

  These thoughts will help prepare you to respond in a peaceful, calm, and loving way.

- **Squeeze them.** If they are banging their head on you, offer to squeeze their head. If they are pinching you, offer to squeeze their hands. If they are biting you, offer pressure on their jawline. If they are kicking you, offer to squeeze their foot or tap on the bottoms of their feet. You want to offer pressure to the part of the body that they are trying to stimulate.

- **Give them an explanation.** Let them know that they do not have to hit, pinch, or head butt you when they feel a build-up in their bodies. That you would be happy to squeeze them whenever they want it. Tell them to give you their hands, arms, or feet when they want a squeeze, and that you would be happy to help them. For example, you could say something like, "You do not have to hit me; if you want some pressure on your hands, I can help you by squeezing your hands. Next time your hands feel like this give them to me and I will squeeze them for you."

- **Give them the sensory stimulation throughout the day.** The idea here is to give them the sensory input that they are seeking throughout the day, so that it does not build up to a moment when they will seek it from using intense energy. I would suggest that you initiate the following activities at least three times a day. As you initiate each activity it is important that you use the Control Protocol we talked about in chapter 1. Each time you go to give your child sensory stimulation, let them see you coming, explain what you are going to do, and look for permission to begin. Remember, it is more important to respect your child's indication of "No" than it is to give them sensory stimulation. If they feel that they have control, they will be more likely to open up and let you give them the stimulation they are seeking.

- Initiate strongly squeezing your child's hands, feet, or head.

- Initiate a bear hug, with you sitting behind your child and wrapping your arms and legs around them so that you can give them a really big body squeeze.

- Initiate rolling them up in a blanket like a hot dog, wrapping them up tightly in the blanket and then rolling them out of it.

- Initiate rolling a big therapy ball over your child. This is a useful way to give a "bear hug" to a bigger or older child. As you roll the therapy ball over your child, put your body weight into the ball so your child gets a really strong sensation.

- Initiate encouraging your child to jump on a trampoline.

- For an older child, 14 and above, I would suggest that you make sure that they get a lot of exercise, such as swimming, jogging/running/long brisk walks, or jumping on a big trampoline, something where they really exert themselves. Do this at least three times a week.

You can experiment with any of the above suggestions. Pick one that you think your child will enjoy the most. While doing the first four suggestions, experiment with the intensity in which you offer the pressure. Slowly increase the pressure while looking to make sure that your child is enjoying it. My experience is that children who are using intense energy because of their sensory needs will like very deep pressure—stronger than you might think.

When your child is using intense energy as a way to protect themselves

You are reading this because your child's signs were mainly in Checklist 4, which most likely means that they are using intense energy as a way to protect themselves in some way. Most children on the autism spectrum have difficulty communicating their wants and desires to us neuro-typical people. Sometimes hitting and punching is the last resort our children use to gain much-needed control in their lives.

For example, I watched a very wonderful and dedicated mother play with her four-year-old daughter named Ellie, who has Asperger's. Ellie was playing on top of a slide with a collection of stuffed animals. She was very intently and exclusively talking to each of the animals and creating a story where the animals were bathing in a river. She was paying no attention to her mom, only to her story and the stuffed animals. Her mom, wanting to get her child's attention, kept trying to get in on the action. First, she moved really close to her daughter and said, "Hey, Ellie, look, I have a lovely duck, hey look, look, the duck is so lovely." Ellie did not respond but kept playing on her own. Then trying harder to get Ellie's attention, she picked up one of the stuffed dogs and moved it slightly, making a "woof" sound. Ellie took the dog and placed it again where it had been previously, all without looking at her mother. This mom loved her daughter and was willing to keep trying to get her child to play with her. Then she picked up the dog a second time and put it on Ellie's head; Ellie took it off and put it down where it had originally been, without saying a word. Her mom again picked it up and slid it playfully down the slide, at which her daughter looked at her, said "No," picked up the dog, and put it where it had been. Her mom again picked up the dog and pretended that it was licking Ellie's face. Ellie pushed it away from her face and said "No." Then her mom rocked the dog in her own arms, saying, "Oh this dog is so happy, it wants to lick your feet." Ellie said "No," and moved her feet underneath her so that her mom was unable to reach them. She then took the dog away from her mom and put it in its original place amongst the other stuffed animals. Her mom again picked up the dog and made the dog tickle Ellie's armpit. Ellie took the dog away from her mom and pinched her mom's arm.

At that point her mom moved away from her daughter looking a little dejected and stopped moving Ellie's animals.

Later, when Ellie's mom and I were discussing the session, she said to me, "I am so glad that you saw that. I don't understand why she pinched me—it came right out of the blue."

We often cannot see that we are actually getting in the way of our children's need to create an ordered, predictable, and controllable world, or that we are not responding to our children's already very clear communication. Ellie's mom sincerely did not mean to be controlling or go against her child—she was just so eager to interact and become part of her world that this was all she could focus on as she played with her daughter. I am sure we can all relate to that. Remember that it is very important for our children to feel a sense of safety in a world that can be very confusing for them. When this world is repeatedly interrupted by others who are unintentionally trying to stop them from doing what they want, our children may feel a need to go to all measures to defend their own wellbeing.

EXERCISE 8.2

To gain a clearer understanding of what is happening just before your child uses intense energy, it will be useful for you to videotape yourself playing with your child. This way you will get to see how you may be unintentionally not giving your child control as you interact and play with them. The idea is to catch a moment on videotape when your child has intense energy so that you can see what happened just before it. Set up a video camera in the room where you interact the most with your child. There is no need to have performance anxiety as nobody will watch it but you. When you are about to spend a few moments of one-on-one time with your child, switch it on. There is no need for someone else to videotape— just pop the camera on top of the TV or shelf where your child cannot reach it. If you do this enough times, you are bound to catch a moment when your child is using intense energy.

- Watch that piece of videotape and look to see if there were any moments when your child indicated that they wanted you to stop or not do something, and at the time you did not realize, so you did not respond to their "No."

- Were you trying to stop them from doing their stims/isms?

- Were you sitting close to them? Maybe so close that you were touching in some way, or sitting right beside them?

As you watch the tape, try to be as compassionate as you can to yourself. You are doing the very best you can, trying to love and help your child who responds very differently than most children. Be excited if you see yourself doing any of the above actions. This is exciting because it will let you know what you can change that will help you and your child have more gentle interactions with one another—you giving her more control, and your child being more physically gentle with you. There is nothing but good news here.

••••••••••••

If this exercise reveals the reason why your child hits then apply the following strategies when you play with your child.

- **Think the following thoughts.**

  ○ My child is doing the best they can to take care of themselves; they are not being bad or mean.

  ○ I am doing the best I can to help and interact with my child.

- **Listen and respond.** Sometimes we can be so focused on "getting" our children to interact with us that we do not focus our attention on listening to what they are already communicating. Shifting your focus to listening and responding to your child will help you see the communications that your child is already giving you, and will help your child not use intense energy as a way to get you to listen. You can do this by paying attention to any movement they might make in response to your initiation. For instance:

  ○ Notice if they move away from you if you move toward them.

  ○ Notice if they move or take away an object just after you touched it.

  ○ Notice if they say "No" or "Yes" to something you initiated.

Once you see these communications you can then respond to them, thus giving your child the control they crave. Do the following:

- If your child moves away from you as you move closer, take note and do not move toward them again. You could even tell them, "I noticed you moved away when I moved closer; I will just stay here for now."

- If you noticed that they move or take away any toys you try to touch, stop touching or moving their toys. You could tell them, "I see you do not want me to touch your toys; that's ok, I will not touch them again. I shall go and get my own collection of toys to play with."

- If you noticed that they indicated "No" to you, you could say to them, "Thanks for saying no, I will not do that anymore."

These are all ways that will help you be more responsive to your child's indications. That way they will not have to use intense energy to seek the control they want over their play or environment.

One additional reason—over-medication

What I share here comes from my experience working with thousands of children and their families. I am not a medical professional (and therefore recommend that any decisions that you make regarding your child's health are only done in conjunction with your physician), but I want to acknowledge that we live in a world where medication is freely and widely given for a variety of different ailments. You only have to switch your TV on to see many ads for medications. Even just ten years ago this was not the case. I have worked with a few families whose children were experiencing a lot of intense energy, of having long outbursts of screaming, hitting, and biting, not only with other people but themselves. These children also had been on three to five different medications for a long period of time—up to five years. Once these children were weaned off some of these medications with the help of their doctors, their bouts of intense energy disappeared—I do not feel that this was a coincidence. If you feel that your child may be using intense energy because they are over-medicated, I suggest you consult with your doctor about weaning your child off some of their medications.

ADDITIONAL TECHNIQUES FOR A TEENAGER OR ADULT

Everything that I have talked about in this chapter applies to an older child, a teenager, or an adult. Below I have added a few more techniques just for the older child who is bigger. Some of you may have children who are a foot taller than you, or up to 100 pounds heavier than you. I have spoken to parents who deeply love their children and at the same time can at moments feel scared for their own physical safety. The techniques below will help you take of yourself and your children. You will need to experiment with the techniques below; any one of them may work, so you will want to find out which one, or which combination, is the most useful for your child and situation.

Create ways to be safe

The first place to start is to set up your environment so that you can protect yourself physically when your child has intense energy. Once you feel you can create a safe place for yourself and protect yourself, it will help you to relax. Feeling relaxed around your child is something I know you want, and you can have that again. Below are things you can do to help you feel more confident that you can take care of yourself physically.

- Since you know your child may use intense energy, be prepared. Get a barrier you can put between you and your child so that you can protect yourself from being hit. This could be a big therapy ball, a big cushion, crash mat, or mattress. Have these readily available in the room you and your child most frequent. When you see the signs that your child gives that mean that they are likely to have intense energy, move calmly over to where your big therapy ball, cushion, or mattress is and put it between you and your child. That way, if your child comes over to hit you, you can put it up so that you do not get hit.

- Try to remove your attention. When your child starts to show signs of intense energy try to take your attention off your child by going to the other side of the room and start to do something else, like reading a book. If possible, leave the room. Sometimes it helps our children if we leave them alone for a little while to work out their intense energy. This was very effective for Olivia.

Olivia, a 16-year-old with autism, was bigger and heavier than me and would have numerous periods of intense energy throughout the day. When she started to show signs of having intense energy, whoever was working with her at that time would leave the room she was in for a while until she worked herself through it. We found that our talking to her and trying to interact with her would only escalate her intense energy. When we left for a while it was easier for her to work through it, and nobody got hurt. We would leave very quietly and say as respectfully as we could that it seemed she could do with some time alone and that we would be back soon. When she relaxed we would return. This is just another version of getting out of the way.

- If you have a child who might follow you around the house and use intense energy, find a room in the house where you can go to protect yourself. Think of a place in your house where you can go where your child cannot follow you. Think of a room that you can go into and lock yourself in from the inside. A bathroom can be a great place for this. When your child shows the signs that they are about to have intense energy, get up calmly and let your child know that you are going to go to the bathroom. Stay there until you feel your child has worked through their intense energy.

  This worked extremely well with Keith, who was 33 years old and would sometimes follow his mom when he had intense energy. She would go into the bathroom at the first sign that he might be getting intense energy. She reported that it worked really well for her. Before she started to use this strategy he would hit her up to five times a day. Once she applied this strategy he would follow her only once a day to the bathroom and bang on the door demanding that she came out. When this happened, his mom would explain to him that she would not come out because she could see that he was having intense energy and did not want to get hit. She would suggest to him that he could go and jump on the trampoline in the living room to get his excess energy out. After a couple of weeks of doing this Keith stopped hitting his mom or following her. She reported that being able to leave and go to the bathroom and protect herself was something that she had never considered doing. Now that she had "permission" to do that, she no longer felt "hopeless or scared" of her son, because she knew that no matter what she could take care of herself.

Say "Stop" and redirect

After doing the exercise earlier in this chapter you will know the signs that your child gives when she is about to use intense energy. Once you see these signs and your child is moving toward you with intense energy, find a strong place inside yourself and, while putting your hand out in front of you like a policeman directing traffic, say "Stop" to your child. in a strong, firm voice. I am not talking about saying "Stop" in an angry way or screaming it, but being like a force of nature. To find a strong loving place inside ourselves that lets them know that we do not want them to hit us or be intense with us. We want to focus this strong energy in their direction so that it "jolts" them, so that they can clearly hear what you want them to do.

Once you have firmly and with great conviction said "Stop," immediately redirect your child to use her intense energy in another way. Do this in the same strong and firm way. You could:

- point to the trampoline and tell her to jump on it

- point to a crash mat or a big cushion and tell her to throw her body into that

- guide her into doing ten jumping jacks.

The two examples below show what the above techniques look like in action.

In the first example, I worked with Tim, a 21-year-old young man who had a vocabulary of about 50 words and would get people into headlocks and punch the side of their bodies. He was much bigger and stronger than me, so I could not afford to get into this position for long. Just before Tim was about to have intense energy his eyes would glaze over and he would start pacing and banging the sides of his body into the walls. I applied the above techniques.

- When I saw the signs that he was about to have intense energy, I moved away from him.

- I put my big therapy ball in front of me.

- When he started to move toward me, I put out my hand and very loudly and firmly said, "Stop."

- He stopped every time.

- I immediately redirected him to jump on the trampoline so that he could get his excess energy out.

All the people who cared for Tim did this. By the end of two weeks, instead of using intense energy on us, he would go straight to the trampoline to jump.

In the second example, George was a 22-year-old man with autism, six foot three, and around 260 lbs. He liked to dress up in suits and ties and look at himself in the mirror while acting out scenes from the movie *Men in Black*, which he loved. This was a wonderful sight to behold. George, however, had no idea of his strength. He would try to jump on our backs for a piggy-back ride or, as part of acting out a scene, would attempt to do a "judo drop" on us as done in the *Men in Black* movie. He was not trying to hurt us, but he did, as he was so big and strong. As a way to protect ourselves we employed the techniques listed above:

- We put out our hands and said "Stop" when we saw the signs that he was about to do a "judo drop" on us or get on our backs.

- We redirected him by providing something else for him to jump onto and "judo drop." We brought in a standing punching bag, and modeled how he could jump onto that instead of us and do "judo drops" on it. We did this by actually jumping on the punching bag ourselves and doing a "judo drop" on it.

After three full days of modeling this for him, he understood what we were asking him to do. On the fourth day he would start to come to us, we would say "Stop" and offer the punching bag, and he would go with it. By the fifth day he was jumping on the standing punching bag without having to be redirected.

A note about diet

Think about your older child's diet. Something that they are eating could be triggering their intense energy. As our children grow older and get bigger they can consume bigger quantities of sugar, additives, soda, and processed foods. All of these can contribute to our children's intense energy. I worked with a mom whose son Patrick was 22 years old and was in a care facility because his intense outbursts meant that she could no longer have him at home. She consulted with me during this period because she wanted to find a way to bring him back home. The first place we started was to change his diet. Luckily, the place he was staying at respected this mom's wishes and let her provide all his meals and snacks. She completely cut out all sugar, dairy products, soda, and sugary/caffeinated drinks. In fact the only drink he was provided with was water. Changing his diet in this way changed everything for him. He was home within the month. Read chapter 12 for more ideas on how to change your child's diet.

Another thought on food is that when your child becomes a teenager their bodies are changing and their need for food increases. Ask yourself whether you are giving your child enough food. Maybe your child is getting "too hungry," which could create feelings of agitation within their bodies that they may not recognize as hunger.

TROUBLESHOOTING

? *My child bangs her head on the wall, so much so that she often has bruises on her head. What do I do?*

I have worked with numerous children and adults who bang their heads. To get an understanding of what it feels like to bang your head I have done this myself, on the wall and the floor. The interesting thing I have found out that it does not really hurt. Our children are very careful to bang their head in the strongest part, which is the front of the forehead, or the sides of the head, thus creating a strong sensation but no pain. I once worked with a lovely four-year-old, who would often bang his head. During my work with him, he would rush over to me, check for my hip bone and then my knee bone, and bang his head in the softest part of my thigh. He was not silly; he did not want to hurt himself. I have watched a seven-year-old boy accidently bang his head on the side of a table, clearly hurting himself (not badly). After having hurt himself he made sure that he never banged his head in that place again.

Our children are very smart. They are not trying to hurt themselves. Head banging can look very painful to us, but remember our children's brains are wired differently to us; what you feel as painful may not feel painful to them. If we adopt the belief that there is a reason why your child is head banging, then we can observe her more clearly looking for signs as to why she may be doing it. If we believe that it is harmful for her, then our immediate response is just to stop it. I am sure you have tried this and she still continues.

When a child head bangs it could be that they want/need pressure on their head. To learn more about this and strategies to help your child read the section of this chapter called "Using intense energy as a way to take care of their sensory challenges."

She could also be banging her head as a way to communicate something to you. The way you would know this is if she banged her head after you had just said she could not have something. For a fuller understanding of this and how to help your child if she is head banging for this reason, please read the section of this chapter called "Using intense energy as a way to communicate their wants." I wish you well in helping your child with this.

? *My child with autism will hit her 18-month-old baby sister. I think she is doing it to get a reaction out of me, but I cannot just ignore it. What should I do?*

The important thing to do here is to take care of your 18-month-old and not give a big reaction to your child with autism. Typically, the child who hits gets either a lecture or time in "timeout" and a lot of attention for hitting. I suggest changing that dynamic by using the following strategy:

- Pick up your 18-month-old, ignoring your child with autism, and quietly leave the room.

- Do not talk to your special child about how it is important not to hit her sibling, as I am sure you have already told her this many times. Talking to her about this at the time may be giving her the attention she is seeking.

- Make no other big issue of the situation.

- Give her the attention she is seeking when she is playing gently with her sibling. At a time when your children are playing or co-operating peacefully together, go to your child with autism and give her much praise and stay and play with her a little. Show her that being gentle with her sibling is the way to get attention and a reaction from you.

This strategy worked beautifully with Wayne. Wayne was eight and had been hitting his younger sibling for three years. His parents had tried everything but nothing had worked. When they first started doing consultations with me I suggested the above strategy. On only the second time his parents implemented the strategy, he said to his parents, "Ok, I will not hit anymore; I don't want you all to leave the room." It was all about the attention he got after hitting his siblings, not the actual act of hitting. Within two days of implementing these techniques this child completely stopped hitting his sibling.

Another important consideration is that usually there is only a limited period of time that we can leave our special children and our typical children alone together in harmony. If we leave them too long, either our special child just takes something that our typical children want, or our typical children don't respect or see our special children's attempts to say "No." Then things can get fraught between them. When I would babysit my special goddaughter and her brother, I knew that I could only leave them alone for a maximum of seven minutes to do something like start to cook dinner or put on the laundry. This was because my goddaughter's brother, who was so super-friendly, would get too close to his sister and unintentionally disrupt her play. If I had to focus my attention on something else, I made sure I put my focus back on the both of them within the seven-minute timeframe. This really helped and reduced any squabbling that would otherwise have taken place. I tried to keep her little brother with me as much as I could. He loved helping me cook. As my goddaughter became more flexible and less controlling, the timeframe they could be left alone together grew.

It's time to become a detective again and find out what your children's timeframe is. For now I would suggest not leaving them unsupervised alone in a room together for longer than this timeframe.

? *How can I not react when my child bites me? It hurts!*

I will pass on to you here what my teacher, Bryn Hogan, Executive Director of the Son-Rise Program, taught me when I asked her the very same question: "If you don't want to get hit again don't react." This very simple sentence has helped me through countless episodes of intense energy. If your child bites you, maybe you cannot stop it from hurting, but you can stop yourself from yelling about it, just as you do at the doctor's or the dentist's. When you are undergoing a painful procedure most of you will "suck it up" and keep quiet. It's no different here.

? *My child really likes to play with my hair, which also includes pulling it.*

Lots of our children are interested in playing with hair. It is a fun sensory activity. If you have a child who finds your hair irresistible and is not always gentle, then I would encourage you to not make it available for your child. You can put your hair up in a ponytail or a bun. I work with one lovely mom who wears a swimming cap when she is playing with her daughter. I know that might sound like a dramatic step, but she says it has completely changed her relationship with her child as she is no longer afraid that her child will pull her hair and can now easily and happily interact with her daughter.

Another useful step to take is to give your child an alternative. Get a doll with long hair or a wig and offer it to your child, letting them know that they can play with this hair instead of yours.

INTENSE ENERGY ACTION CHECKLIST

- ☐ Be aware that our children hit not because they want to hurt us but because they are trying to take care of themselves.
- ☐ Consider the four major reasons why our children hit:
  - ☐ They are trying to communicate something to us.

- ❐ They want to see us react to their intense energy in a big, interesting way.

- ❐ They are taking care of their sensory challenges.

- ❐ They are trying to protect themselves in some way.

❐ Notice the signs that your child gives 15 minutes before or during the times when they are using intense energy.

❐ Find out which checklist group your child's signs are in (see earlier in the chapter). It will either be group 1, 2, 3, or 4.

❐ Do the following if you are in checklist group 1:

- ❐ Move slowly.

- ❐ Explain to your child that you do not understand their intense energy.

- ❐ Move fast to other forms of communication, such as verbal communications, sounds, and physically moving you.

- ❐ Move out of the way when you see the signs that your child is about to have intense energy.

- ❐ Give your child an alternative if they want something that you cannot or do not want to give them.

- ❐ Do not give your child the thing they had intense energy for.

- ❐ Make sure you ask your child to communicate either verbally or nonverbally if you decide to give the thing to them. Tell them you gave it to them because they used this new way of communicating, not because they hit you.

- ❐ Be persistent and consistent with using the above techniques each time your child uses intense energy.

❐ Do the following if you are in checklist group 2:

- ❐ Change your reaction to your child's intense energy.

- ❐ Change your reaction to a "non-reaction." Be quiet, calm, and non-interesting in your response.

❏ Explain calmly just once that you want your child to be gentle, and that you do not understand what their hitting means.

❏ Give a big, fun, over-the-top reaction to all the times when your child is gentle.

❏ Do the following if you are in checklist group 3.

    ❏ Think: *My child is hitting me in an attempt to take care of their sensory system. Their actions are not connected to their love for me, or their respect toward me. I can help my child by giving them more sensory input to help them balance their bodies.*

    ❏ Squeeze the part of your child's body that needs sensory input. This could be the head, the feet, legs, or hands.

    ❏ Explain to your child that they could give you the body part that they need squeezing and you would squeeze it for them. They do not need to hit or kick you to get that stimulation anymore.

    ❏ Initiate different sensory input throughout the day so that you child's energy does not build up into intense energy.

❏ Do the following if you are in checklist group 4:

    ❏ Think: *My child is doing the best that they can to take care of themselves—they are not being mean to me. I am doing the best I can to help and interact with my child.*

    ❏ Videotape yourself with your child in the hope you will record an intense energy episode.

    ❏ Compassionately watch the tape to see if you missed any signs from your child that they wanted you to either stop what you were doing, stop touching their toys, or stop talking in some way.

    ❏ Listen and respond to your child's cues of "No" more as you play with your child.

❏ Employ techniques for an older child who is bigger, such as a teenager or adult:

- ❐ Create a safe environment for yourself:

  - ❐ Have a big therapy ball, cushion, crash mat, or mattress that you can put between you and your child.

  - ❐ Leave the room when you first see the signs that your child is going to use intense energy.

  - ❐ Find a place in your house you can go where your child cannot follow you, such as the bathroom.

- ❐ Redirect your child's energy:

  - ❐ Put out your hand in a stop sign and loudly and firmly say "Stop" as your child comes toward you with intense energy.

  - ❐ Redirect your child to jump on the trampoline, throw themselves onto the crash mat, or do another strong physical activity.

- ❐ Check your child's diet.

This is going to be an adventure for you. I hope that you now feel equipped with enough tools to confidently help your children when they have intense energy.

TOILET TRAINING

Are you smiling? Are you ready for the adventure of toilet training your child? If you have been waiting, here it is finally—clear, specific ideas and techniques that will help you to help your child to fall in love with using the toilet! This is going to be different! I will not be suggesting that you use the traditional method of asking your child to sit on the toilet every 30 minutes or every hour. Using this method our children can feel pushed, and being interrupted from their current activity so many times actually makes the toilet less appealing to them. We are going to create the opposite experience for our children. One that is easy, relaxed, fun, and altogether wonderful for you and your child. This is going to be a great adventure into toilet land! For those of you who have already toilet trained your child but have toilet-related questions, go straight to the "Troubleshooting" section at the end of this chapter.

LET'S START WITH OUR ATTITUDE

For our children we are the ambassadors of the toilet and the world of pee and poop. If we are not excited about the toilet, then why should they be? Are they not perfectly happy wearing diapers, and being cared for and cleaned by you? It is usually our agenda, we adults who want our children to get out of diapers and move on to the more adult, independent world of the toilet. It is up to us to make this experience as fun and as exciting as possible, so that our children will find it hard not to be interested in sitting on the potty. *This is all about our attitude to the toilet.*

When was the last time you came out of the bathroom jumping up and down sharing your joy with the world about the fact that you just peed in the toilet? If your answer is just yesterday, then you are on your way to making the toilet fun and exciting for your child; if your answer is "never," then your first step will be to adopt some new thoughts and beliefs about the joy of the toilet.

The toilet, pee, and poop are wonderful things!

I was having lunch with a dear friend and her lovely six-month-old baby boy. While we were eating we heard loud and amusing gas noises coming from his direction, and then the distinct smell that a poop had arrived in his diaper. His mom's face fell, she looked a little embarrassed, and she said, "Phew, that's disgusting," scrunching up her face disapprovingly as she picked her baby up to change him. As she proceeded to change her baby she carried on talking to him, saying, "I would rather you did not do such stinky poops; they are not fun for Mommy, and they are gross and yucky."

I have seen numerous other situations where similar scenarios happen between caregiver and child. The overriding message is poop is stinky and horrible. Pee, although less offensive than the glorious poop, is often met with a sigh or displeasure when it falls anywhere but the toilet itself.

This way of dealing with poop and pee has been carefully passed down from generation to generation. Why this should be is not obvious to me. Some, if not all, of you will have experienced what it is like not to be able to pee or poop. Also you will have experienced the glorious relieving and most wonderful moment when after a couple of days of not being able to poop you actually manage to—you know what I am talking about—didn't you secretly want to go and tell someone of your amazing feat and celebrate a little?

Helpful beliefs to adopt

- Poop and pee are important bodily functions for our bodies.

- They are signs that my child's body is healthy and that our process of elimination is working, without which we would be in serious trouble.

- If our children did not pee and poop they would be in pain.

- Smelling these fluids helps me know that I have an opportunity to offer my child the toilet.

The above thoughts will help you adopt a more celebratory attitude toward your children's poop and pee. Having a celebratory and welcoming attitude will help your children move more easily toward the experience of getting to the toilet. If they sense that you do not like what they are doing, they are more likely to move away from the experience. If we can communicate to them that what they are doing is fabulous and exciting, they are more likely to adopt this attitude themselves and move more toward the idea of doing this exciting thing in the toilet!

LET GO OF ANY "PUSH" OR "PRESSURE"

You may feel outside pressure to get your child toilet trained. Our children are not allowed to attend certain nurseries, schools, or activities if they have not achieved this skill yet. Some parents confide in me that they think other people think they are a bad parent because they have not managed to toilet train their child yet. This may translate into us pushing or needing our children to sit on the toilet. When our children feel pushed they push back by becoming controlling. Your child has ultimate control over when and where they are going to pee and poop. This is just something that we cannot control; therefore it is even more important than ever that our children feel that they have control over when and how they pee and poop and we feel relaxed and easy about it.

If you resonate with feeling outside pressure to toilet train your child quickly, I would like to suggest that you can let that go right now. Don't let anyone else dictate to you how long it "should" take you to toilet train your child. Your child is unique. Don't put a time limit on this adventure. It's between you and your child and nobody else. Focus instead on the fun you are going to have together as you embark on presenting this life-long skill to your child. Focus on being easy and relaxed; it does not have to happen right now, as no matter how old your child is, you do have time to help them. Let the toilet games begin!

If you have already spent a lot of time focusing on potty training and feel that your child is just not getting it, check in with yourself to see how you feel about it. Parents have expressed to me that they feel "frustrated and annoyed" because their efforts have not succeeded. When we feel frustrated or annoyed about something, we may begin to get attached to the outcome of needing it to change in order for us to feel happy. Then out of the need for change we start pushing our child. There is nothing wrong with feeling frustrated that your child won't pee in the toilet; it just is not helpful when we are encouraging our children with autism to use the toilet. Even if you do not "show" your frustration to your child by shouting or yelling or forcing them in any way, they will know how you are feeling. Our emotions show up in a million tiny ways; our voices get harsher and our actions more jerky. We know when someone is hiding their frustration under a forced smile, and so do our children. In short, things get tense. Have you ever tried to pee or poop when you are tense, or feeling under pressure to hurry up and get on with it? The opposite usually happens—you clam up and shut down.

If you resonate with feeling frustrated with the efforts you have already implemented with your child, I would suggest that you let go of toilet training for a while, for at least a month. If your child has created a control issue around it, letting go of this on your part will help ease the situation. Oftentimes taking a break can completely change the previous dynamic; our children are quick to note any internal attitudinal changes in us. Taking a break will also help you de-stress about the issue and let go. Then when you restart you do so with a clean state and the benefits of having read this chapter and being armed with clear, effective, no-pressure strategies.

If you, the school, a babysitter, or Grandma has either dragged, forced, or made your child go to the toilet, then your child probably has the "I don't like the toilet" mindset. To change this mindset for your child I would also suggest that you take at least a three-week break from toilet training and then restart with the new pressure-free strategies in this chapter.

HOW DO YOU KNOW WHEN YOUR CHILD IS READY?

Toilet training is something that every child can achieve. It is possible for your child no matter how old or how severe their challenges. But your timing is important. Start toilet training when your child has passed at least three of the following milestones. This way your child and you are much more likely to succeed, and the process will take a shorter period of time.

- They are two and a half years old and above.

- They have an interactive attention span of at least two minutes. An interactive attention span is not how long they can interact with an object, but how long they can focus their attention interactively with you. For instance, they are looking at you and involved with an activity that includes you, such as a chase, or tickle game, building a tower together, or drawing or having a two-minute conversation together.

- They show some awareness that they can feel that they need to use the toilet by:

  ○ hopping around and doing the many unique versions of the "I need to pee" dance

  ○ going off to poop in a quiet corner of the house

  ○ asking for a diaper to pee or poop in.

- If they pee when they do not have a diaper on, they notice that the pee is falling down their legs, rather than just carrying on as if nothing has happened.

Special note: If your child has reached these milestones but is also extremely controlling, meaning that their most frequent answer to any request is "No," then perhaps it is not the time to focus on toilet training, but instead focus your energy on helping them become more flexible. Once your child has relaxed their need for extreme control, you can begin your focus on toilet training, which will be met with more flexibility and openness on the part of your child. For information on how to help your child with their flexibility, see the Son-Rise Program Developmental Model by going to the following link: www.autismtreatmentcenter.org/contents/other_sections/developmental _model.php.

START AT THE BEGINNING
Find out what your child's natural rhythms are

You can do this by answering the following questions:

- How long after they drink do they pee?

- How long is the average time between each pee?

- What time of day do they usually poop?

- How many times a day do they poop?

The best way to find this out is to create a "potty diary" over a period of a couple of days. The best times to do this would be either on a school holiday or three-day weekend break from school.

Write down the time of day they poop. Most of you will probably know when your child poops. A lot of children tend to do this at a similar time each day. If your child does not seem to poop at the same time each day or does so multiple times, just write the time of each poop down and over a couple of days a pattern usually emerges.

Write down the times of day your child pees. Diapers make this a little harder to know. In order to find that out be prepared to take the diaper off and dress them in underwear and trousers so that you can see when they pee. Write the times down in your potty diary. Cross-reference this against the times they drank and ate so that you can see how long it takes for them to urinate after eating or drinking.

Once we know this information then we can start to encourage our children to sit on the toilet 15 minutes before they usually need to go. This is much more effective than the trend in the autism world to get a child to sit on the toilet every 30 minutes or every hour. When you use the information you gathered from your potty diary you will be taking your child to the toilet when they actually need to go. This helps our children associate the feeling of needing to go to the toilet with an actual trip to the toilet. We are also more likely to catch a pee or a poop in the toilet. I have seen so much more success with this method. Each of our children is unique—let's tailor our approach to them.

Things to have before you begin
Potties

If you have a young child, purchase a few small potties so that you can have one in easy reach when you notice your child needs to pee or poop. If you live in a multistory house, have one upstairs and one downstairs. If your child spends a significant part of the day in a particular room, have one in that room. This will be very useful, making toilet training as easy and relaxed as possible by having a potty in easy reach. This way you can avoid a control battle of pulling your child to the bathroom by bringing the potty to them. We want this experience to be fun, easy, and relaxed.

Child-friendly toilet seats

For the actual toilet you can get seats that you put on the toilet to make the seat smaller and more suitable for the younger bottom; that way our children can sit comfortably without the feeling that they might fall in. You can buy these in different materials such as plastic, or decorated with different Disney characters/animals/birds or soft and furry material. Think about what types of materials your child moves toward easily and happily, and buy one that you think will be appealing to them.

Camping potty

If you have an older child, seven years and above, then you can get a camping potty that you can purchase from any camping shop. This is a potty that is big enough for an adult to sit on. You can lock it. There are two different kinds: one that flushes with water and one that flushes with chemicals. As our children can be very sensitive to chemicals I would suggest that you get the one that flushes with water. Again, put this in a room that your child likes to frequent the most. Or a place in your house which would make it so that you and your child would always be in easy reach of either your bathrooms or the camper potty.

Tarp/tarpaulin

Find or purchase some tarpaulin or ground sheets. They are great because they are movable and easily washable! Use them to cover any carpet or special flooring that you have in your house while you are toilet training your child. This will help you feel more confident and comfortable in the face of any accident your child may have during the day.

Two-part potty

Small potties usually come in two parts: the part that you sit on and then the container that holds the pee and poop. You can pull the container out so that you can dispose of the pee. Even if your child is too big for a potty, get one so that you can use the container to catch pee in. This is especially useful for boys. Let's say your child has started to pee; you can catch it easily in this container, and then both of you can go and pour it into the toilet. This is a great tool and stepping stone to getting the pee in the toilet.

Pick a date to begin

Pick a date in the future to start your potty training. Make sure you pick a date when you are not due to visit your family or have them visit you. If you have a partner, it would be helpful if they are around; if not, ask a friend or another family member if they would help out, by either picking up some of your groceries so that you can limit the times you have to go outside (where you will have to put a diaper on your child) or by taking care of your other children.

Be 100 percent internally ready

Be rock solid in your commitment to stay the course in helping your child through the many accidents they may have on their journey to successfully being potty trained. If your child has accidents, this is actually something to get excited about because it is a sign that they are on the path to being toilet trained. When we learn to ride a two-wheeler bike it takes us many times of falling off before we arrive at that magical moment where we find our balance and can pedal away, never to fall again. Just as you would cheer on a child who fell off his bike while learning to ride, cheer on your child for nearly getting it in the toilet when they miss. After each accident they are one accident closer to being potty trained.

A checklist to know you are ready to begin

Begin when you have got all your potty ducks in a row—meaning:

- ☐ You have the important information about when your child is most likely to poop or pee.
- ☐ You have everything you need: potties and ground sheets.
- ☐ You have a date and time in mind when you can begin the process.
- ☐ You are internally 100 percent ready.
- ☐ You are excited to begin the process.

THE TOILET PLAN
Let your child know exactly what going to the bathroom entails

There is great secrecy surrounding what actually happens when an adult locks himself or herself in the bathroom. They go in silently, and come out again making no announcements about what they got up to in that room, looking just the same as they went in. Start to share what goes on in there!

- Show your child what goes on in the bathroom. For the girls have them in the bathroom when you pee and let them see the stream going into the toilet—how else are they going to know? For the boys, all you dads out there, model peeing in the toilet. If you are a single mom and do not have a partner, ask an uncle or have an older sibling brother demonstrate his amazing ability to pee in the toilet. After you poop, instead of getting up and flushing straight away, have your child come in the bathroom and let them see the poop in the toilet. Excitedly tell them how great it felt to poop and how happy you are to have pooped in the toilet!

- Verbally explain to your child exactly what poop and pee is, and why it is useful for them to use the toilet. Remember that we want to talk to our children believing that they can understand us. Of course, as you speak to your child, do so in a way that is appropriate for their current age. Use all the real words for things, like penis, vagina, pee, or poop, instead of the mystique of "number one" or "number two," "down there," "tiddle," or "thingy." There is nothing to be embarrassed about—this is a completely natural and healthy activity. Explain:

  - how your body digests food, and that the poop and pee are the parts of the food our bodies do not need

  - how the pee comes out of the body through a hole and into the potty

  - how the poop comes out of the body through a hole and into the potty

  - how it is taken out into the sewer and disposed off

  - how great it is that they will not have to wear diapers anymore, that they will have more comfort without the wet of the pee and the stickiness of the poop against their skin

  - how using the toilet helps keep us fresh and clean

  - how comfortable and fun it is to wear big girl and big boy underwear.

As you explain all of the above, remember you are the ambassador for the toilet. Share this great information in a fun and enthusiastic way.

Make going to the bathroom a big event in your house

- Whenever you feel the need to go to the toilet, after making sure that you have no visitors in the house and that it is just you and your family at home, announce to everyone loudly and clearly that you have that special feeling in your tummy that means that you are so lucky because you get to go to the toilet! It is important that this is expressed with delight and great anticipation.

- Once you have done the wonderful deed and have come out of the bathroom, have the other people in the house come to praise you! Do not force your child with autism to come along; if all the other members of your family come they just may feel the urge to come and see what is going on. Plan with the other members of your family to come and applaud every time someone declares that they need to use the potty. If your child does not like the sound of clapping but loves music, then create a simple potty song that they could come and sing instead. A potty song could go like this:

  > Oh I am going to the potty, hip hip hip hooray!
  > I am sitting on the potty, oh what a lovely day!
  > I get to pee, and wipe and flush, hooray hooray hooray.

  If you are a single parent and you do not have any other children, no worries, you can still do this. Instead of other people coming to cheer you and sing or clap, go to where your child is in the house, and praise, clap, and sing the potty song to yourself. This will mark just as well the wonderful occasion of you using the toilet for your child.

- Make potty or toilet certificates that can be awarded each time a family member uses the potty. Design the certificates to be motivating to your child. If your child likes Thomas the Tank Engine then have him on the certificate. If your child likes to talk about the weather, then write interesting facts about the weather on the certificate. These are to be prized and displayed by your family.

- This is not about getting your child to do anything or asking your child to do something concerning the toilet—this is just about making it fun and a big event in your house. This must be a sincere activity, because you cannot fake things with your children; if you are doing this but not really enjoying yourself, they will know. Get behind the fun of this. You have nothing to lose—just a good time to be had by you and your family.

Decorate the potty or toilet

You want to make the toilet or potty an interesting and motivating place for your child to be and visit. Take one of the motivations from the list you created in exercise 4.1 and use it to make your potty or toilet more motivating for your child. If your child loves a certain character decorate it with stickers and pictures of that character. If your child loves pieces of string decorate your potty with string, if they love softy furry things, decorate it with fax fur. If your child loves cars you could build a road from paper leading up to the potty or toilet, or a runway, or a train track, or the yellow brick road and so forth.

Take the diapers off!

Diapers today are wonderfully advanced, so much so that our children can wear them and not feel in the slightest bit wet or uncomfortable. On the one hand, this is great because we want our children to feel comfortable and the occurrence of diaper rash is greatly reduced. On the other hand, unfortunately it does not help your child to feel or notice when they pee and we cannot see when they do this. So potty training will go so much faster if we take the diapers off. Of course, you will still use them any time you have to leave the house or during the night.

While I am suggesting taking the diaper off, I encourage keeping your child dressed in big girl or big boy underwear and tracksuit bottoms that can easily and quickly be pulled down.

This is where the tarp/ground sheets come in. Put them down to cover the carpets and sofas that your child may be sitting on while they are diaper-free. This way you do not have to be concerned about ruining your carpets or furniture and can keep a relaxed, easy attitude when your child has an accident.

Break it down

Learning to independently use the bathroom consists of eight stages:

1. Noticing when you have to go to the bathroom.
2. Pulling down your trousers/underwear.
3. Sitting on the potty.

4. Peeing or pooping.

5. Wiping yourself.

6. Pulling up your trousers/underwear.

7. Flushing the toilet.

8. Washing your hands.

Focus on one at a time. Some you will have to teach, and some your children may just do without much prompting. Ask them to do each stage; they might surprise you and do it easily straight away.

One mom was shocked to hear that I thought her son Aleem had no issues with dressing himself or using the bathroom—all eight stages. I just asked him to do it and he did! His mom had never asked; she had been doing it for so long for him it had not occurred to her.

You don't have to do the stages in order; for instance, if your child cannot do stage 2, I would do that for him and work on stage 3. The priority is using the toilet—it is ok to pull your child's trousers down and wipe them at first; eventually they will learn all these steps.

Ask your child to sit on the potty or the toilet

Remember that our main objective is getting our children to want to sit on the potty independently of us. That means we want to make it a stress-free experience for them. Keeping in mind that it is important to give our children control (chapter 1), we do not want to physically force our children to sit on the toilet by dragging them there; we want them to go there under their own free will. That does not mean that we cannot hold their hand or pick them up and take them into the bathroom, but only with their permission. If they move away from us or say no, respect that and try some of the suggestions below. Toileting is something we cannot force our children to do, as it is something that is completely in their control; thus while giving our children control is extremely important, it is even more important around toileting.

When to ask them to sit on the toilet

- 15 minutes before they usually pee or poop. You will know this from the information you gathered in the "potty diary."

We want to ask 15 minutes before so that we have time to get there in an easy and relaxed way. We will have time to ask in a variety of different ways.

- When your child is doing their own version of the "potty dance"—crossing their legs, jiggling their legs, or holding their genitals.

- When you see that your child has already started to pee or poop. The wonderful thing about taking the diapers off is that you will see this now, and thus have many more real opportunities to offer the toilet.

- When they show interest in either the potty, the camper potty, or the toilet, by either looking at it, walking over to it, or touching it. That means we have to keep an eye open to see this. If they just walk past the bathroom or by the potty, offer the toilet. If they glance over in its direction, offer it.

How to ask

- **Verbally**—Just ask them any fun way you like. You could say one or more of the following suggestions:

  ○ "Honey, it's time to go visit the potty—hooray! Let's see if we can pee or poop—I wonder which one it will be."

  ○ "It's potty time again! Come on, let's see who will get to the toilet the quickest."

  ○ "It looks like you really want to pee or poop. Come with me to the toilet so we can put it in there."

  ○ "I have brought the potty to you because it's potty time-yippee! Let's sit on it."

Have their favorite character or puppet tell them that it is potty time. Maybe it is a figurine of Elmo, a shark puppet, or a toy vacuum. In my experience our children sometimes find it easier to respond to our requests when they are made through a puppet or figurine. Don't forget to use the voice of the character when you do this!

- **Take their hand**—You can do this as you verbally ask or after you have verbally asked and have not received a response from your child.

  Go over to them and explain that you are going to take their hand and walk with them to the toilet. If they allow this, head to the nearest toilet. As you walk with them, be sensitive to whether they are coming with you freely; if they pull away from you, let them know they have control by letting go of their hand.

- **Pick them up**—As you go to pick up your child it is very important that you use the Son-Rise Program Control Protocol in Chapter 1. Explain that you are going to pick them up and take them to the bathroom so that they can sit on the potty. Tell them in a fun and excited way! Look for permission. If they move away from you, struggle, or resist being picked up, it is very important that you give them control and do not pick them up. We do not want to have any control battles with our children, but this is even more important with toilet training.

- **Go into the bathroom by yourself**—You can do this while you are asking your child; sometimes you actually going to the bathroom helps them decide to go with you. If your child has not responded to your verbal or physical request then tell them that you will see them in there and go yourself. Once in the bathroom, make something fun happen in there so that your child might want to come and see what all the commotion is about:

  ○ Make some noise: sing a song your child likes, play the harmonica, or bang a drum.

  ○ If your child likes particular scenes from a movie, start acting them out in the bathroom—loudly enough so that your child may hear.

  ○ Take some object into the bathroom with you that you know that they like. If they like to play with string or play dough or cars, let them know that you and a ball of string or some cars are going into the bathroom and that you both hope that they join you soon.

- ○ If your child likes visual stimulation, like things flying through the air or dropping in front of their eyes, then make things fly around the bathroom—or out the bathroom door.

The idea is to find a way to give your child a good reason to visit the bathroom.

- **Be persistent**—Ask more than once, ask more than twice; it may take many times of you asking before your child responds. Stick with it. Believe each time that you ask and they do not respond that you are one step closer to the time when they are going to respond. Our children find responding to us and the world, and doing everyday things like sitting on the potty, so much harder than their neuro-typical peers, so it stands to reason that it will take them a little longer to catch on to the idea. Let's not give up on them; stay the course and give them more opportunities to succeed. The moment we stop giving them opportunities we rob them of the chance of being able to learn.

  Now, this does not mean that you have to stay doing this all day. There is no precise science as to how long you keep offering the toilet to a child who is not responding or even showing you that they are taking in what you are doing. I would say as a guideline if your child has not verbally or nonverbally said a clear resounding "No" then keep going using the varied techniques listed above for a minimum of five minutes. It is my experience that even when a child has shown no clear interest in me they are aware of what I am doing and saying. I want them to know that I think that using the toilet is a fun and wonderful thing that they could do; the more I show them this the more likely they will start thinking about trying it themselves. I want to have done it so much that my child might lie in bed at night thinking, "Boy, Mom really does love going to the bathroom, maybe I should try it."

  If your child has clearly stated "No," then respect that and let them know that you will try again in three to five minutes.

- *Want* **your child, versus** *need* **your child, to sit on the toilet!**—Asking persistently in the ways outlined above will only work if we can do it from a place of passionately wanting our children to sit on the toilet without "needing" them to. We are needy when our happiness, feeling of success, or wellbeing is reliant on our children doing what we have asked them to do, in this case sit on the potty. Make sure it is really ok with you if they decide not to.

Our need for a particular outcome that is not happening as fast as we want it to usually freezes our brains. Suddenly we cannot think of any other ideas to help our child sit on the potty and we may feel that they will never get it. This soon becomes a self-fulfilling prophecy. Funny how the moment we get unhappy or needy we can't think of another thing to do. What we think and how we feel as we play and encourage our children is so, so important. If you notice that you are feeling attached to having your child sit on the potty, take a break: take ten minutes out and make yourself a cup of tea. As you are drinking your tea contemplate the following thoughts:

○   There is no rush; no matter how old your child is they can be potty trained.

○   Your house was not built overnight, but brick by brick; the same applies to your child learning new skills—request by request.

○   You are the best person to help your child; you have the strongest relationship with your child, and you know your child the most and have the most time to give to your child.

○   You and your child are doing the best that you can.

Let go of the goal of having your child sit on the potty, and enjoy asking your child to come to the toilet. Focus just on this request, and the fun of enticing them there.

Modeling going to the toilet

•   Whenever you need to go to the toilet, let your child know and come with you.

- Have different stuffed animals and characters go to the potty. You can act this out in front of them with the little potty.

  ○ You could keep it simple by walking a teddy bear over to the potty, lean him over the potty, and have him take a pretend pee, making a pee noise. While you are doing this, make a deep pretend voice for the bear who might say, "Oh, I really need to pee, it must have been all that berry juice I drank." After peeing he (the teddy bear) might say, "Oh, that felt so good, and I am glad that I can pee in the toilet like a grown-up bear; that way I don't have to wear diapers, and I keep the forest clean." Then praise Mr. Bear for being such a clever bear. Don't feel that you have to get your child to watch you or participate in this little game you are playing, but do praise them and encourage them if they choose to.

  ○ If your child does not really like regular toys you can do it with inanimate objects, like trains, cars, strings of beads, and magnetic letters or numbers. With a little imagination everything can use the toilet.

Use your child's motivations

Use your child's motivations by weaving the toilet into things they are already interested in. You can weave going to the toilet into any game that your child is already playing with you. This way your child gets to think and explore the concept of sitting on the toilet within subjects and activities that they are already interested in. You can do this at times when your child does not actually need to go to the toilet. For example:

- Let's say your child likes to act out scenes from Disney movies, maybe *Toy Story* or *Beauty and the Beast.* Have your character stop and go to the toilet. Maybe Buzz Lightyear has to make a pee in outer space and you and your child have to figure out together how to make a space toilet.

- Maybe your child likes to draw—you could start to draw a person sitting on the toilet.

- If your child likes to spell, you can spell out the words "toilet time" or the sentence "T likes sitting on the toilet."

- If your child is into math and numbers, you could calculate how many times a week, month, or year the average person uses the toilet.

- If your child likes to talk about a particular subject, like storms or Michael Jackson, you could introduce the subject of going to the toilet by wondering what type of toilet Michael Jackson had, or how you could go to the bathroom in the middle of a tornado.

Celebrate, celebrate, celebrate

Never underestimate the power of celebration. We all like it! When we were children we did either what got us the most attention or the most celebration, and maybe for some of us that has never changed.

Of course, I know that you will be very sincere and passionate when your child uses the toilet for the first time! I am sure that your celebration will be big and genuine. One thing we might not think to focus on is to celebrate all the little steps our children take before they get to the final destination. Below are some suggestions of all the steps to celebrate along the way.

- Celebrate everything our children do in relation to the toilet. Praise them:

  - when they look at the toilet

  - for entering the bathroom when you ask them to

  - for touching it

  - for sitting on it

  - for getting a poop or a pee in the potty

  - for noticing that they have just peed or pooped

  - for telling you that they needed to use the toilet

  - at each stage of pulling up and down their trousers, wiping themselves, flushing the toilet, and washing their hands.

- Use a variation in your voice.
  - ○ Celebrate loudly in a cheerleader voice.
  - ○ Celebrate sweetly and tenderly like you do when you kiss them goodnight.
  - ○ Celebrate by whispering your celebration.
  - ○ Celebrate by singing a rock song or a lullaby.
  - ○ Celebrate using funny voices, like Donald Duck, Mighty Mouse, and Popeye.

TROUBLESHOOTING

? *My child will not let me change his diaper—it is always a fight.*

This is most likely a control issue. Doing the following when attempting to change your child's diaper will help.

- Explain to your child in detail why it is important for him to have his diaper changed:
  - ○ that you are trying to help him not get a diaper rash from having poop or pee on his skin for too long
  - ○ that a diaper gets full and can only hold a certain amount.
- Give your child warning before you attempt to change them. They may experience diaper changing as too sudden a transition from one activity to another and feel the need to push against it. Give them a countdown before you change them: give them a ten-minute warning, then a five-minute warning, and then a two-minute warning; this way they are able to prepare themselves for the event.
- Experiment with different ways of changing them. In my experience of changing many different children of varying ages, each child likes to have it done differently. One style I find effective is having a certain place where you always do it where your child brings himself. For example, I would lay down a towel on the floor, get the wet wipes and a clean diaper and lay them next to the towel, and then pat the towel

as I ask my child to lie down so that I can change their diaper. This way your child can see a visual representation of what it is we are asking them to do and they can come under their own steam. Or I do it while they are standing up and absorbed in their own activity; maybe they are looking at a book, or lining up their objects on the table. They do not have to break from their activity. Experiment with different ways to see if one would work better.

Maybe it is a sensory issue; are your hands too cold? Maybe they feel rough on your child's skin? Our hands might be sticky from cooking or have glue on them; maybe your child is moving away from the feel this has on their skin. It could be another sensory issue that is not actually related to the changing of the diaper. Maybe we have on a perfume or a hairspray that is overwhelming for our child and it is that they are moving away from. Put on your "detective" hat once more and investigate to see if it is a sensory issue for your child.

? *My child smears his poop and eats it.*

I was consulting with a lovely mom of a five-year-old boy with autism. She talked with great animation and enthusiasm about her son until she started to broach the subject of her child smearing and eating his poop. When she began to talk about this she whispered and did not look me in the eye. When I asked her why she was whispering, she said it was because she did not want anyone to know, as it was so shameful. She was also sure that her son was the only child that did this. Shame can be a very isolating emotional experience. So, the first thing to know about this is that you are not alone; your child is not the only child on the planet who does this and there is nothing to be ashamed of. This activity is done by both those who are on the spectrum as well as neuro-typical children. The only reason that you think you have the only child who does this is because no one talks about it. So let's talk about it now. What to do:

- Decide to feel good about this. Instead of seeing this as disgusting, let's keep in mind what we talked about earlier— that poop is a wonderful thing our body is doing. That we are glad our children can poop. We can still come from this place as we teach our children that poop is great but not something we eat. This will make the situation easier for you and for your child.

- Make it harder for them to do this activity.

  o Put your child in clothing that makes it difficult for them to stick their hand into their diapers and retrieve their poop. For example, you can put them in a onesie and then in a jump suit that fastens at the back or dungarees. Or one-piece PJs where you can cut the feet off so that you can put it on backwards so the zipper is at the back. That way they will not have immediate access to their poop.

  o When you are changing your child's diaper give them something else to busy their hands with so that their minds are not on the poop.

  o Let nothing distract you from changing the diaper quickly so that your child does not have time to grab any poop. Not the phone or your other children—let nothing take your attention away from the deed in hand. Sometimes we unwittingly give them the time to grab their poop by being distracted by the phone or our other children.

- Get your child tested for a dietary deficiency. Some of our children may want to eat their poop because they have a mineral deficiency. Ask your doctor to test your child to see if this is the case.

? *My child will smear his poop in the middle of the night.*

I have worked with many families where this is the case. In 95 percent of these cases it was all about what happened once the child had smeared. The parent would clean up their child by giving them a bath and spend up to 30 minutes or more with their child. This became motivating for their child to continue to smear because they liked to take a bath and have their parents' attention in the middle of the night. Smearing was just a way to get that. Once the parents took away their attention and the fun bath time, the children stopped smearing. What might help you to achieve this? There are two possible ways to try:

- If your child only smears a little I would suggest leaving the poop and not cleaning it up at all. This is very effective. There are numerous examples in my experience of children never doing it again once they see their parents are not going to come in. I have never heard of any child dying or getting sick because they have a little poop on them. How often have you fallen asleep with baby poop on you without even realizing it? Letting your child fall asleep with poop on them does not make you a bad parent; it is your intention that matters. You are doing this to help your child learn that poop lives in the potty and is not to be played with.

- If your child smears a lot and by leaving them it will be literally all over their bedroom and you will probably have to spend the better part of a day cleaning it, then try entering your child's bedroom in a very quiet fashion—do not engage or talk to your child. The idea is not to make it fun—but that does not mean that you make it unpleasant for your child either; just go for a neutral effect. Instead of giving your child a bath, just wipe them down with wet wipes and leave as quickly as possible.

? *My child is fully toilet trained. He will play with his poop while it is in the toilet bowl.*

If your child can independently sit on the potty and will use this as a time to smear then give them an alternative substance to play with. Poop has a certain texture and is strong smelling—put a bowl of a substance with a similar texture by the potty. It could be silly putty, plasticine, play dough, or mashed-up bananas; add into it an essential oil—pachouli is particularly strong smelling. Tell your child that playing with his poop is not healthy for him but he can play with this substance instead as long as he wants to.

This method proved very successful with Ali, a 12-year-old mid-verbal child with autism. He was completely toilet trained but would play with his poop in the toilet bowl when he was alone in the bathroom. His hands were starting to become very irritated from the contact with the poop. His parents felt that they could not be with him every minute. We decided to put a bowl next to the toilet with the plasticine in. We explained to him that his hands were irritated because of the contact with the poop and that he could help heal his hands by playing with the plasticine rather than the poop and that we were going to leave that for him to play with instead. His parents modeled this for him by giving him the bowl of plasticine any time they were actually in the bathroom with him, and reminded him each day of its presence. By the end of the week he had stopped playing with his poop!

? *Even though my child will pee in the toilet, each time he poops he asks for a diaper and does it in there instead of the toilet.*

Pooping is an intense physical experience for us all. I can only imagine that it is a more intense sensory experience for our children on the autism spectrum. A lot of our children have digestive tract challenges, which can result in them either having a lot of diarrhea or constipation; thus pooping is more of a challenge for them. We all have our own rituals and ways we like to poop.

The most effective way to deal with this issue is to take away the diapers; stop buying them and get rid of the spare ones you have in your house. The slow way is to pick a date in the future where you tell your child that as they are getting bigger it is time for them to begin to transition from pooping in the diaper to pooping in the toilet—make this a happy, fun declaration. That in two weeks' time, they will only have one diaper a day to use. Tell them that they can ask for it and use it at any point in the day, but once it is used there is no more until the next day. Then after doing that for two weeks, let your child know that the diapers are now all done.

The fast way is to go straight to the stage of having no diapers in the house. If you have a younger sibling who uses diapers that are a similar size make sure that they are in a place in your house that your child with autism does not have access to. You can get rid of the diapers in two ways, the slow way or the fast way; the choice is yours, as they are both effective.

Once you get to the stage where there are no diapers in the house at all, do the following:

- The day before you use the last diaper decorate your toilets in a way that you know will motivate your child. For example, I know of a lovely family who decorated their toilet with *Dora the Explorer* stickers—their daughter loved it. Another tied a series of bows around their toilet as their child loved ribbons. One created a speech bubble coming out of the toilet that said: "Welcome Max's poop! I am excited to receive the very first poop from Max! Thank you Max." Followed by a big smiley face.

- Stand clear and solid in your decision not to have diapers in the house. If your child senses that you are not sure about your decision, they will hold out for the diaper. If they feel that you are rock solid, they will move on.

- When they ask for a diaper, let them know in an excited and congratulatory voice that you do not have anymore as they now are so clever that they have graduated to the toilet—that your toilets are now ready and excited to have your child's poop. Then let them know that you decorated the toilet for the occasion and ask them to come and have a look.

- Then model sitting on the toilet and request your child to do the same.

- If they say no, then tell them that they do not have to poop right at this moment; they can go at any time that they please, but the diapers are no longer available.

- It is important that you give your control at this time and do not force them in any way to sit on the toilet. I would tell them they can poop on the toilet whenever they are ready and then leave them alone in the toilet. I have so many stories of children pooping in the toilet once they are alone and no one is telling them what to do.

- They may start to cry, believing that that will move you to get a diaper for them. Know that your child is not in any danger or distress—they are just using the tantrum in an attempt to get a diaper. If you have read chapter 7 you will already know how to respond to the tantrum. It is no different in this case. Tell them that they have graduated from the diaper to the toilet and even if they cry it won't make the diapers come back—that they can now poop on the toilet.

- Know that they will survive and move through this transition, that you are helping them make a useful transition for themselves that will help them function in the social world.

? *My child will disappear to another part of the house and poop alone.*

This may be because they do not want the people around them to react in the loud "Oh, did you do a stinky poop?" way that they may have in the past, preferring to retreat. If that is the case, then just inform your child that you think that their pooping is a wonderful healthful thing and it is ok for them to do it around you and in the bathroom.

Sometimes our enthusiasm gets in the way! Pooping is a big sensory experience and it may be that our children want to be left alone and be in private, and the only way to achieve this is to go off on their own. If you sense, having read so far, that your trying to engage and interact with your child as they try and poop is not working, experiment being quieter. One lovely girl I worked with was clearly holding in her poop and not responding to my fun and lively requests to sit on the toilet. So I changed tack; I lowered my voice and my energy, told her that she could take all the time she wanted pooping in the bathroom alone, and I left and sat quietly in the other room giving her some space. Seven minutes later she sat on the potty; it took her 15 minutes to finish pooping. It obviously took time and concentration on her part, and was easier for her when I was not around.

If you have changed yourself in the ways above and your child is still pooping away from you in another part of the house, investigate and see if you can find out what it is about this place that is appealing to your child. One family I was working with had a boy of six who would always poop next to the air-conditioning vent. I suggested to the family that they put a fan next to the toilet. The boy started pooping on the toilet soon after that. Something about the cool air helped. Remember, there is always a reason as to why our children are behaving in their unique way—our job is to believe that and then attempt to find out.

If you cannot see what the reason is maybe they started this off by accident one day and now they have become rigid in wanting to always do it that way. First put a potty in the exact place that they are pooping in; let them know that you put it there so that they can poop in it. Every couple of days move the potty slightly closer to the bathroom; these slight changes may help your child accept the change of pooping in a different place.

? *My child will not wash his hands after he uses the toilet.*

If your child will not wash his hands in the sink, start with taking a wet washcloth to wherever he has run to after using the toilet. Using the Control Protocol of explaining, giving warning, and looking for permission, wash his hands with the cloth or a wet wipe. This will help him get used to the fact that we wash our hands after we go to the bathroom.

Once you have done that for a while, next time you are in the bathroom, start to run the taps before your child had finished using the toilet. Make it fun for your child to want to come over to the sink before they leave the bathroom.

- If your child likes bubbles, fill the sink with a little water and make some bubbles.

- Get some soap in the shape of their favorite character.

- Fill the sink with a little water and put some trains at the bottom and ask your child to rescue the fish.

- Model washing your own hands with excitement. Afterwards you could mention how clean they feel and how nice they smell.

? *He will not wipe himself after he has pooped.*

Successful wiping takes time, practice, and patience. According to Dr. Christopher Green typically developing toddlers do not wipe themselves for at least a year after they have learned to poop on the potty, and then they take a year to master the art. The advice here is to keep encouraging your child to do this in a fun and easy unattached manner.

? *My child keeps peeing on the floor—he does it on purpose as he looks at me and laughs when I tell him not to.*

This sounds like a button push. Remember, we talked about button pushing in chapter 6. This is when our children do something just so

they can see our reaction. The clue that leads me to believe this is that
he is looking at you while he is peeing on the floor. This indicates he is
more interested in what you are going to do about him peeing on the
floor than the actual act itself. The first thing you want to do is notice
your reaction to him peeing on the floor. Do you shout "No" and rush
over to him in a dramatic way? If you do, it is most likely this is the
dramatic response that he is looking for. Next time your child pees on
the floor do not respond in any way. Wait a few minutes before you
even clean up the pee. Then the next time your child does something
that you really want him to do, like look at or talk to you or actually
pee in the toilet, give a really big dramatic positive response to it. If
our children want us to react in a big dramatic way, let's do it when
they do things we want them to continue to do. See chapter 6 for lots
more on button pushing.

? *My child stands up or crouches while pooping on the toilet.*

Rejoice and be happy that your child has created a way that is effective
to use the toilet. I would say—Does this matter? As long as he is using
the toilet successfully why does it matter whether he sits, stands, or
crouches? We actually don't know how every person uses the toilet
once they are in the privacy of their individual stall, or in the privacy
of their home. Different cultures have different kinds of toilets; in some
countries the correct way of using a toilet is to crouch above a hole in
the ground. Celebrate that they are using the toilet successfully and
let this be. It is obviously working for them. Later, when our children
are able to connect with us more deeply or understand things more,
we can invite them to sit as well.

? *My child takes all their clothes off before peeing or pooping on the toilet.*

I have seen many children want to take all their clothes off to go to
the bathroom. Whilst this is fine in the safety of your own house it
is more challenging when you are in a public toilet or at school. The
way to help your child with this is one step, or one piece of clothing,
at a time. In my experience, children who do this have one thing in
common: they have challenges with different kinds of textures on their
skin and can be tactile-defensive. Sound familiar? If this is the case,
I would suggest that you start the brushing protocol with your child

(see Chapter 11), which will help them with their underlying sensory challenges.

So what do I mean by helping them with one piece of clothing at a time? Get your child used to wearing something when they sit on the potty. You might first start with something very small—as they sit on the potty put on a pair of funny glasses yourself and offer them the chance to wear a pair—or you could start with a hat or a special pair of potty socks. Once your child accepts this then add another piece of clothing; start small and then work up to the bigger stuff like trousers.

? *My child had potty skills and now has completely lost them—why is that?*

This is not uncommon for our children. Our children's bodies are different and react differently to their experiences. This could be due to one of a number of things.

It could be because there are added stresses going on in their current lives. Check to see if anything has changed in their external environment. Maybe they have moved to a new school, or there is construction happening close to your house. If you see that it could be related to environmental changes, do what you can to ease the challenge. If, for example, your child has just started a new school, be patient with your child while they adjust. Make their time outside of school calmer and more predictable—this will ease the transition. Know that once they have adjusted, you can start to toilet train again. The second time around will not be nearly as time-consuming or as challenging as the first. They have not lost the skill—they are just not able to concentrate on it due to other challenges.

Perhaps they have just taken a leap in their social development. Maybe your child is in a therapy program and they have been working on language and have started to speak more, or have lengthened their interactive attention span; because your child has focused their attention on learning this skill, potty training may take a second seat for a while. Once this new skill has been integrated, your child will pick up their potty-training skills again.

Above all be patient with your child; know that they are doing the very best that they can.

? *If my child learns to pee on the potty, will they be able to transfer it to the toilet easily?*

My answer to that is yes. I have worked with over a thousand different children and adults, with varying diagnoses, and I have never come across a situation where a child will pee in the potty but not in the toilet. The concept we want to help our children have is that their pee and poop goes into a container and that they keep themselves clean and fresh.

The most important thing to remember as you embark on your toilet training adventure together is to have fun and be easy. If you apply the techniques in this chapter, your child will learn to use the toilet. The important thing is to relax and have fun together trying. We don't know how long your journey will be, but you will get there in the end. Enjoy the process!

TOILET TRAINING ACTION CHECKLIST

- ❏ Decide that the toilet, poop, and pee are great, wonderful things.
- ❏ Create a "potty diary."
- ❏ Buy everything you need—potties, tarp, camper potty, etc.
- ❏ Pick a date to start toilet training.
- ❏ Verbally explain to your child what the toilet is all about.
- ❏ Model using the toilet to your child.
- ❏ Make going to the toilet a big event in your house.
- ❏ Take the diapers off.
- ❏ Ask your child to sit on the potty. Ask in a variety of different ways.
- ❏ Use your potty diary to know when to ask your child.
- ❏ Ask them when they show interest in the potty, toilet, or camper potty.
- ❏ Ask them when they do a version of the potty dance.

☐ Ask them when you see they are already peeing or pooping.

☐ Be persistent. *Want* versus *need* them to sit on the toilet.

☐ Weave the toilet into games you play with your child.

☐ Celebrate every attempt your child makes toward using the toilet!

Chapter 10

SLEEPING

SLEEP IS GOOD FOR ME, AND GOOD FOR MY CHILD

Sleeping can be a great challenge for our children on the autism spectrum. Studies show that between 44 and 83 percent of children with autism have some form of sleep challenges (compared to 10–20 percent of typically developing children).

When our children do not sleep that means we do not either! Sleep is essential, not only for your child but also for you. Without sleep our common sense goes right out the window. Problems can escalate as we are unable to create a reality checking balance; we can even "invent" problems where there are none. We can be irritable, irrational, and easily move into temper. This is not helpful when parenting a child on the autism spectrum who wants predictability and consistency. It is also not helpful for your marriage, or for your health. It is not surprising that sleep deprivation is considered an effective method of torture, driving people into confusion and even madness.

Sometimes you may feel that your life is just too difficult, that you just cannot manage your everyday with your child. I wonder how this might change after two weeks of good sleep, or a month of sleeping through the night? The chances are you would feel very different about your child and your situation! Your head and body aches would decrease. That brain fog you have lived with for years would clear. You would probably find the energy that has been eluding you and manage your everyday with your child with more ease!

A month of sleeping through the night! Doesn't that sound good! Is it not music to your ears? For those of you who are seriously sleep deprived I bet it is something you would choose over tickets to the World Cup Final or winning the lottery! If the answer is no, then you do not want it enough to get it. Our sleep is so often dependent on how much our children sleep. Between what we think and what we imagine our children are thinking we give ourselves 101 reasons to not sleep and stay up with our children. Do any of the following thoughts sound familiar to you? Maybe your children are verbal and actually tell you these things, or maybe you believe that these are what they are saying based on your interpretations of their actions.

Things you may imagine your children are telling you:

- I am up, so you should be up.

- I am not tired enough to go to sleep yet.

- I am too scared to sleep by myself.

- I will not like you if you leave me to sleep by myself.

- I think you are really mean for not staying up with me.

Things you may believe about your child:

- My child will not go to sleep unless I lie with her for the first five hours.

- My child will make a lot of noise and wake up the neighbors.

- My child will make a lot of noise and wake up her little sister.

- My child will stay up and sleep all day instead of going to therapy if I do not sleep with her.

- My child will be physiologically scarred for life if I leave her to cry herself to sleep.

- My child will wake up really early if I move her bedtime to an earlier time.

- My child is too scared to sleep on her own.

We can give ourselves many reasons not to change our children's sleeping pattern. If you use the techniques and strategies in this chapter you will find it is much easier and quicker than you imagine. After doing these strategies, parents often tell me that they wished they had done it sooner.

Joanna, a six-year-old girl diagnosed with PDD, would stay up for 36 hours at a time, never wavering in her energy. If her mom tried to go to sleep herself, Joanna would pull the covers off her and say, "Stand up."

If she did not stand up she would pull her arm or hair until she got out of bed. She would then demand that she put the TV on and get her some food. Her mom felt that she had no choice but to do what her daughter was demanding.

Ian, a five-year-old boy diagnosed with Asperger's, would declare forlornly with one tear running down his cheek, "Where has all the love gone? There is only hate here now," whenever his parents suggested the idea of him sleeping by himself in his own room. He was brilliant at being dramatic and pulling on his parents' heartstrings.

Alfie, a 14-year-old boy with autism and epilepsy, would stay up until 2am every night. His mom was very concerned about leaving him in his room alone in case he had a seizure, so she would stay up with him playing until he fell asleep each night. She had three other children to take care of and she was up at 6am each morning; Alfie, however, slept on until 10am, waking refreshed, unlike his mom.

All three of these families had their children sleeping through the night within a week of applying the techniques in this chapter.

Some of the techniques outlined below may be familiar to you. They are effective and simple; there is no magic or rocket science here. They do however require a commitment on your part to follow them through and not give in to an easy night or a quick fix. That's why it is important to start to really want and visualize a good night's sleep, for you and your child. Imagine how it would change your life and help your child!

Imagine putting your eight-year-old and younger to bed at 7.30pm, your 14-year-old and younger to bed at 8.30pm, or an older young adult to bed by 9.30pm. Then having that beautiful silence that fills the house once your children are asleep. Peace. Where no one is asking you for something. No need to take care of someone. A few moments to yourself, where you could take a bath, or get on with all the things you need to do without another demanding your attention. Imagine all the amazing benefits your child would get from a regular night's sleep.

Think of the benefits for your child. Our children are like their neuro-typical peers in that sleepless nights will mean that they get cranky and irritable and more challenging to manage. Unlike their typical peers it may also mean that they become more repetitive, controlling, and rigid. Lack of sleep could also exacerbate their sensory challenges, maybe making loud noises or touch more unbearable. Helping them sleep through the night will help them attend more to their schooling or therapy. It will be easier for your child to focus, to listen, and to handle the unexpected as their stress level, compounded by lack of sleep, will be lowered.

A study published in the journal *Sleep* found that when we are sleep deprived we have a greater difficulty understanding facial expressions (van der Helm, Gujar and Walker 2010). Our children already have challenges understanding social cues such as facial expressions, which is further exacerbated by lack of sleep.

When we have a vision of what we want for our own lives and the lives of our children, we have something concrete to move toward and create. The more we want something to change the more likely we will follow through with the necessary steps to make it happen, even when faced with the determination and persistence of our crafty children.

PUTTING YOURSELF TO SLEEP IS A LEARNED SKILL

This is a skill we all had to learn, which means it will be important to give our children the opportunities to learn it. This realization took me by surprise. There are things we need to teach our children that are obvious, like how to ride a bike, eat with a knife and fork, or play soccer, but putting themselves to sleep was not one that was on my list. In the Son-Rise Program, we have successfully helped hundreds of children learn to *put themselves* to sleep. Our children simply never learned that skill, and we can easily teach it. Many of us do not give our children this opportunity. Instead we do some version of the following routines:

- Rocking them lovingly to sleep in your arms.

- Lulling them to sleep by putting them in the car and driving them around.

- Letting them fall asleep in front of the TV, or on the sitting room couch.

- Lying down beside them with your arms stroking their back.

- Literally being their pillow or mattress.

- Reading them a book until they are sound asleep.

Once they awake to find themselves not in the car or on the couch or without their Mom or Dad, they go immediately to find the thing that will help them sleep again. Which is you! It makes logical sense that they would come and wake you up. If they had learned to put themselves to sleep they would most likely turn over and put themselves back to sleep. In order to help them learn this skill we have to give them the opportunity to do this by leaving their bedroom before they are completely asleep.

Teach our children that nighttime is for sleeping

When our children wake up at nighttime and indicate that they want food or drink, some of us may go downstairs and get them a drink or cook them food. By doing this we are teaching them that nighttime is a time to eat. They may ask us to sing a song, or want to see bubbles; if we oblige we are teaching them that nighttime is a time to play. Our children can sometimes be at their most interactive and affectionate during the night. This may be due to the fact that nighttime is often when our houses are quiet, with the rest of the family sleeping and they have our undivided one-on-one attention. I can understand wanting to take advantage of that; however, it teaches our children that nighttime is for playing. If you teach your children that only sleep happens at nighttime, they will be more likely to sleep. A well-slept child and parent will have more opportunities to play during the day than a tired one.

EXERCISE 10.1

Find out what you are teaching your child about nighttime by taking a moment to think about what you do with your child in the night. What do you say to them? Do you play with them, sing to them, feed them, hug and kiss them, read stories, or watch TV with them? Do you give them a bath, crawl into their bed, or bring them into your bed? Write down exactly what you do; reflect on what you wrote and see what you are teaching them about nighttime.

_____

_____

_____

_____

_____

_____

....

FOOD CAN PLAY A PART IN OUR CHILDREN'S SLEEPING PATTERN

Dairy products, sugar, and eating just before you go to bed are three of the most common factors that contribute to sleep disturbances.

Dairy products

There have been studies that have linked a sensitivity/intolerance or allergy to casein, a protein that is found in all dairy products, to night waking, in particular night laughter or night talking. If your child wakes up in fits of laughter over nothing that you are party to, or babbles or chats to herself, I would suggest that you try eliminating dairy products from her diet for at least three months and see if that makes a difference. (See chapter 12 for ideas on how to do this.) If your child is sensitive to dairy it can also cause lethargy during the day, causing them to sleep during the day and be up at night.

Sugar

Sugar is a stimulant. It increases our children's energy tenfold. I know that you have seen this with your own children. You give them sugar and everything speeds up. You yourself might reach for something sugary as a way to give yourself an energy boost. A teacher once told me that on "treat" days, which were days when a child brought in a birthday cake, or it was Halloween or another holiday, they would hand out the sugary treats only 20 minutes before they sent the children home so that they did not have to deal with the children's "hyperactivity" and the chaos that 20 children "on sugar" creates. Needless to say we do not want to give our children something that will help them stay awake just before or near bedtime. Please read chapter 12 for more on sugar, and how to take sugar out of your child's diet.

I worked with a family who had a 12-year-old girl with autism who had never slept through the night. Her family were at their wits' end having not slept a full night in 12 years. She was very partial to sugar. Her parents and I went through everything she ate—it all contained sugar. Her parents agreed to experiment with slowly taking sugar out of her diet. Once they had successfully eliminated this completely from her diet, she started to sleep through the night for the first time in her life. Her parents employed no other strategies—this was the only thing they did.

Eating just before bed

Feeding our children just before they go to sleep can produce two things:

- **Energy surge**—food is supposed to refuel us and give us energy to run, skip, walk, and dance. This is not what we want when putting our children to bed.

- **Indigestion**—making it hard to fall asleep. You might have experienced that yourself, wishing you had not eaten a heavy meal so late.

Additives, soda, caffeine, and chocolate are all stimulants that would be wise to eliminate from your child's diet to help with sleeping issues. Eating any of these items just before bedtime will make it near impossible for our children to fall asleep.

My godchildren had what is called a "last call for food." This happened after their evening meal and no later than an hour and a half before their official bedtime. Once this was over there was no additional food offered or given before bedtime. Their parents have used this since they were very young and they have both always slept through the night with ease (including the period of time when my goddaughter had her Son-Rise Program).

CREATE A ROUTINE AND STICK TO IT

Our bodies respond very well to sleeping routinely. I wake up at 6am whether my alarm goes off or not, simply because my body is used to waking up at that hour. I start getting tired at 10pm, the time I usually go to sleep. My body knows my pattern because it is a routine that I have developed over time.

The National Sleep Foundations says, "The #1 tip for good sleeping habits in children is to follow a nightly routine. A bedtime ritual makes it easier for your child to relax, fall asleep and sleep through the night." (Sleep for Kids, ND) The magic to a bedtime routine comes from using it. The 8 secrets outlined below will help you do just that.

Eight secrets to a successful sleeping routine

Secret 1: Explain the new set-up to your child

With this new mindset and resolve we want to communicate this new set-up to our children. The day before and the day you decide to change your bedtime routine explain in detail to your child what is going to happen. Spend some time explaining to them that if they wake in the night you are not going to come in and lie with them any more as you want to help them learn to put themselves back to sleep. Tell them that they get to sleep the whole night in their own beds. Tell them that you are still here in the house and love them very much and that you know that they are going to be able to do it, that you will see them in the morning and have a lovely breakfast. Use a fun, upbeat tone while explaining this. Then give them a "bedtime buddy." Bryn Hogan, my great friend and fellow Senior Son-Rise Program teacher, created the idea of "bedtime buddies." You buy a large or mid-sized soft teddy or doll. Each of you, both Mom and Dad, takes a T-shirt that you have slept in for a couple of nights and puts it on the "bedtime buddy." This is so great because your child's new bedtime buddy will actually smell of you, bringing a little of Mom and Dad into their own bed.

Secret 2: Set the scene

It's one hour before bedtime and our children have just finished their last call for food. Start to create a peaceful and calming atmosphere in the house. You are letting your child's body calm down and helping to prepare them for sleep. Turn off any computer games or TV that may excite. Turn on some peaceful music; "Sleepy Baby" from Brain

Technologies is specially designed to promote sleep (see http://advancedbrain.com/music-for-babies/sleepybaby.html). Put this on at a low volume in the background and see if you notice a difference, not only in your children but yourself. Play peaceful quiet games with your children; stay away from games such as tickle, and rough and tumble. These games can energize and over-excite our children. If they ask for these games, explain to them that it is nearly bedtime, so you would love to play tickle or rough and tumble tomorrow. Now you would love to cuddle with them and read a book, or do a puzzle.

If it is summertime draw some of the curtains, letting them know that bedtime is approaching; if it is winter, dim the overhead lights, or turn them off and put on a smaller lamp. Forty-five minutes before bed, start to either go upstairs or move to their bedroom sleeping area. This will give you time to give your child a bath before the final stages of the bedtime routine. Each of these steps will become indicators for your child to register it is bedtime and they may even cause the body to become sleepy.

Secret 3: Allow your child to cry

Allowing our children to cry in the short term will help them sleep in the long term. Our children's crying is usually the Achilles heel of the bedtime routine. The most common reason our children do not have a regular bedtime or sleep through the night is because we find it hard to listen to them cry for us. I understand this. Sometimes our children can cry for an hour or more before falling asleep. We know that as soon as we go in, and either get into their beds or have them get into ours, they will most likely stop crying and go to sleep. Or if we go to them and stay with them, they will stop crying and then the rest of the household will not be disturbed. This, however, is just a temporary band aid, and will only ensure that this continues for years to come. The solution is to help them sleep by themselves by not going to them when they cry.

Some of you may fear that if you do not go to them they will think we have abandoned them, or do not love them. I would like to suggest a different mindset—one that will help you stand strong in your conviction that letting your child cry is not a mean or terrible thing but actually is a loving and helpful act for your child. It always helps if we can think of the bigger picture—which is that you love your child. Your child knows that you love them. You have not abandoned them. Most of our children can't even conceive of a world where we would not be there. You are right here. You have provided a wonderful warm and caring home for your child. They are safe, and all is well. Crying themselves to sleep a couple of times will not harm them or your relationship. It will actually help them and your relationship. As I talked about before, helping your child sleep through the night will help them focus and connect more to you. It will help them learn new things and process the things they have already learned. All of these benefits will help your relationship with them. The best thing you could do for them in this moment is to teach them to fall asleep by themselves. If we give them the opportunity to do so, they will learn this. Letting them cry in the short term will serve them much more in the long term.

Another point to keep in mind. I was helping one mom with her worries about letting her child cry in the night and not going to him and taking him into her bed. When I asked her why she felt she could not do that, she said he had enough to deal with and he deserved the comfort of his mom during the night. Afterwards she burst out laughing. I asked her why she was laughing. In reply she said, "Who am I kidding? Half the time in the middle of the night I am tired and grumpy, hardly the comforting mom I just talked about." We chuckled together at the reality of this. We are tired and understandably we are not at our best in the middle of the night. This realization helped her to resist going to her son in the middle of the night and to change his sleeping routine.

In short form:

- It is ok if she cries, it will not scar her for life. We have all at one point or another cried ourselves to sleep and woken up the next day perfectly fine.

- It is an important life skill she is learning that she will use every night for the rest of her life.

- By letting her cry and giving her the opportunity to put herself back to sleep I am helping her get rest and rejuvenate her body, which will promote health and leave her rested for her therapies or school.

- I have made my child's room safe so I know she is ok.

- My child is loved, well fed, and well taken care of; she knows this and will not hold this moment against me.

- I will get through this moment and so will she.

This means not going into our child's bedroom when they wake up and cry for you in the middle of the night. It means not lying down with them until they fall asleep—which means leaving their bedroom when they are sleepy but not fully asleep so that they can practice putting themselves to sleep.

Secret 4: Take your child back to their bedroom

If your child wakes up and comes into your bed in the night, it can be so tempting to just let them stay in your bed. Sometimes they get in and fall immediately back to sleep. You are tired and it seems easier in the moment to do that. I have been there too! Go back to your bigger picture. You want them to be able to sleep through the night independently in their own bed. This will serve the best in the long run. If they are coming into your bed in the night, it is a sign that they still need you to be there to put themselves back to sleep. You will not always be there. Help them learn this by taking them back to their own room immediately. As you do this you can remind them that they are now going to sleep in their own bed all night. Keep doing this as many times as they come in. It may take only one time for your child to get this. It may take 20 times the first night you are taking them back to their room. Keep doing this; if we persist our children will get it.

Francis was three years old and had always slept in his parents' bed. They implemented all the strategies in this chapter. They had to take him back to his own room 30 times the first night, only six the second, and none at all on the third night. Since then he has slept in his own room all night. It takes less time than we think. Think about it this way: a couple of nights of being up is a small price to pay for a lifetime of your child sleeping through the night independently in their own room.

Some of our children will just leave their bedrooms after you have finished their bedtime routine and left their bedroom. First consider your reaction when they leave their rooms at night:

- Are you playful with your child when they leave their room? Do you chase and tickle them back into bed? Do you let them stay downstairs for ten minutes when they come down? Do you have a full conversation with them, or hug and rock them as they sit on your lap?

- Do you react in a "negative" way, by shouting at them, giving them a long explanation as to why they cannot come out of their room, or showing your frustration and displeasure in a dramatic way? This could have turned into a button push (see Chapter 6) where they want to come out just to see your reaction.

All the reactions listed above, or other versions of the same, make it fun and interesting for your child to leave their room. The idea is to make it completely boring and uninteresting for your child by remaining calm and easy and keeping your fun and playful side only for the daytime by doing one of the following:

- **Take your child back to their bedroom each time they come down.** Do this in an easy but uninteresting way. This means: do not engage in a lengthy conversation with them; do not engage in any attempts by them to play a game with you; and do not get them food or water, or let them watch any TV. (Of course, if they are sick then tend to any needs they might have.) You may have to do this up to 30 times in the course of one night, but if you do it religiously straight away each time, it usually only takes three or four nights for them to change this habit. If your child is one of those who keeps coming out frequently, it may serve you to stay right outside their room for a while so their trip outside of their room remains uninteresting. Remember, if you invest the time now you will reap the benefits later. This method is effective no matter how old your child is. In the initial few days that you start doing this make sure that you keep activity in the rest of the house to a minimum. If your child really likes TV or computer games, do not have anyone in your house using the TV or computer while your child is learning to stay in their room and put themselves to sleep—they may be leaving their rooms just so they can have one more glimpse at the TV or chance at the computer.

- **Put up a gate at your child's door.** This works great for younger children. Make sure that it is high enough so your child cannot climb over it.

- **Lock your child's bedroom door.** This is a quick and easy method to keep your child in their bedroom. This is just another boundary to help your child get their much-needed sleep. We all create boundaries for our children. We lock the front door at nighttime so that our children do not leave the house alone and get hurt. For some of you, locking your child's bedroom door at night may be no different. You may have a child who gets up at night and goes down into the rest of the house and plays with appliances that are dangerous for them. Your child may do this without waking you, so it would prove necessary and helpful to your child to lock their door to keep them safe. If you want to do this, know that you are doing this to benefit your child, not to punish them in any way. Let them know that their door will be locked and why this is so. Put a camera baby monitor in your child's room so you can see what is going on in there. Make sure your child's room is completely safe for them (see Secret 6). If your child is potty trained put a camping potty (see Chapter 9) in their room so they can use it if necessary. This is to help them stay in their room and learn to sleep through the night.

If you have an older child or adult who you can have a conversation with and can reason with them, create a "staying in their room" deal. Give them control over what time they are to stay in their room; give them a choice of three times. Make all the times you give be times you want them to be in their room. Giving them the choice will help them feel that they are in control. For example, tell them that now they are older they can choose when they are to go to their bedroom and stay in there for the night out of the following times: 8pm, 8.30pm, or 8.45pm. Also have them choose the time in which the lights will be turned off, for example 8.30pm, 8.45pm, or 9pm. If you have a child who will constantly change their mind, then let them know that once they have picked a time then it will be that time for the whole month; at the end of that month they can choose again if they wish from the same timeframes.

The above negotiations will help your child feel that they are choosing their bedtime, and thus help them stick to their agreements more easily instead of railing against your authority.

Secret 5: Make their own room a fun place to be

Redesign your child's bedroom to make it a fun place for them to be. If your child has been sleeping most of their nights in your bedroom, then they may be either unfamiliar with their own bedroom or it may just have become a storage place instead of an actual bedroom.

Explain to your child that they are old enough now to sleep the whole night in their own room and you are going to make their room warm and cozy for them. Maybe you buy a new comforter or duvet cover with your child's favorite character, car, or football team on it. Maybe you get them a night-light or a new soft toy to sleep with, or some new bedtime books to read to them. Show these things to your child with great excitement, while you are actually in their bedroom.

Secret 6: Make their room safe

Take a look at your child's bedroom from the point of view of safety. As we have already discussed, we will not be going into our child's room when they are crying in the night, so we will want to know that they are super safe. Thus it is very important for you to make their room very safe. So consider the following:

- If your child is a climber, where will they most likely climb? Then make that impossible to do. You can do this by taking out chairs or dressers that they may climb on. If your child's bed will give them access to climbing, then take the frame out and have your child sleep on a mattress on the floor—futon style.

- If your child likes to chew on things, make sure there is nothing your child can chew on and break leaving a sharp edge.

- Make sure there are no small items your child may eat and choke on.

- You can also fit their bedroom with a camera baby monitor so you can see what they are up to when they are crying in the night without actually physically showing up. This will give you extra peace of mind.

Secret 7: Let them fall asleep by themselves in their own beds

We want to leave our children's bedroom before they are actually asleep. That means that if you used to read to your child until they were asleep, now still read but just stop before they are asleep. If you used to lie down with them, sing, or rock them until they were asleep, still do this ritual but just stop and leave the room before they are asleep. If you don't stop and leave them to fall asleep by themselves, you rob them of the opportunity to learn this important life skill.

Secret 8: Make no exception

The magic of a sleep routine is the consistency with which it is carried out. There may be times when you think that it would just be easier if you let your child sleep in your bed "just this one time." Often that "one time" becomes the pattern. If we are to help our children change their sleeping pattern, it is important that we give their bodies a chance to acclimatize to that change by giving them consistent opportunities to do just that. It may seem like "just one time" to you, but it may disrupt their body rhythms or their belief that you now mean it when you say it is bedtime.

There is one circumstance where it would be prudent not to stick to your bedtime routine—if there is some kind of emergency such as a fire. Which of course is obvious! Even when your child is sick you can still stick to your routine, and have them sleep in their bedroom. If you need to tend to your child during the night, such as giving them medicine or helping them if they are having a coughing fit, make a bed up for yourself in their room. That way you can still nurse them through their illness and keep them used to sleeping through the night in their own bed without you. Many parents tell me that their children get off their bedtime routine and start to sleep in the parental bed again after a bout of illness. This does not have to be the case.

If you are to achieve the dream of having children who sleep through the night, change your "just one time" mindset to "I will do what it takes to help support this new routine."—You can do it!

Some helpful sleep routine possibilities

You can pick any one of the following routine time outlines and use them, or you can create a routine of your own. It does not really matter what you do; the effectiveness lies in how you do your routine, and in the eight secrets outlined above. In this section I have suggested different times and different bedtime activities; you can choose one exactly as I have written it or adjust the activities to what you think will suit your child best. Even if your child is two to five years old, read the other age group activities I suggest, as these may be more suited to your child. For the younger age groups I have suggested that you give your child a bath before bedtime—the warm water can (serve to) help soothe your child. However, you can bath your child at any time of the day—it does not have to be part of the bedtime routine.

For a child 2–5 years old

5pm	Dinner
6.15pm	Bathtime
6.40pm	Read two stories, sing one song, arrange all their soft toys in a certain order, lie down with them and cuddle them for five minutes, and kiss them goodnight.
7pm	Turn off the light and leave the bedroom.

For a child 6–8 years old

5.30pm	Dinner
6.45pm	Bathtime
7.10pm	Lie with your child in their bed while you both listen to some soothing music played quietly in the background, rub their feet or head.
7.30pm	Turn off the light and leave the bedroom.

For a child 9–14 years old

6.00pm	Dinner
7.00pm	Last call for food
7.30pm	Bathtime
8.10pm	Read three stories to your child. You could hold your child's hand or stroke their head if they allow you.
8.30pm	Turn on some background music, turn off the light, and leave the bedroom.

For a child older than 14 years old

6pm	Dinner
7pm	Last call for food
8pm	Start to set the scene for bedtime.
8.30	In the bedroom, you read them stories, or leave them to read a little by themselves if they can read, or look at magazines or picture books if they cannot, or leave them to play a little in their room with their preferred calm item of choice (no TV or DVDs).
9pm	Come back, say goodnight, and turn their lights out.

THE STORY OF JOANNA

Joanna, the six-year-old girl with autism we met earlier in the chapter could stay up for 36 hours at a time, or only seemed to need one hours sleep a night. Her mom would attempt to go to bed herself, only to be woken up by her child shouting at her until she got out of bed, went down stairs with her, turned the TV on, and gave her a bowl of cereal. Joanna did not want her mom to interact with her, but she wanted her mom to sit on the sofa while Joanna divided her attention between dropping "magnetic letters" in front of her eyes and watching TV. Each time her mom tried to get up she would scream and pull her down onto the sofa. Her mom stayed thinking that she had to.

Joanna's mom simply could not go on with getting so little sleep. I helped her create a good routine and she was determined to stick with it. It worked perfectly. She did the following strategies:

- Not going to her in the night when she cried.

- Helping her stay in her bedroom by putting up a gate.

- Making her room super safe.

- Making her room fun for her by getting her some My Little Ponies, which she loved just for bedtime.

- Making no exceptions. Always putting her to bed in her own room at 7.30pm.

- Leaving her to fall asleep by herself.

On the first night she was put to bed at 7.30pm, when her mom left her room, she was wide awake, showing no signs of being sleepy. Her mom left anyway, teaching her that playtime was over and that nighttime had begun. Half an hour later she started to cry; she cried for her mom for approximately two hours. She stopped crying but she stayed awake playing in her room until 2am. Her mom found her asleep in one corner and picked her up and put her in her bed. The next day she did not cry for her mom; she played in her room, and was found asleep in the same corner at midnight. Over the two weeks she slept earlier and earlier, until she slept from approximately 8pm until 7am.

Nighttime was no longer interesting to her. Her mom, TV, and food were no longer available to her. In their absence the only interesting thing to do was to go to sleep. The more she slept, the more her body got used to sleeping and the more she was able to sleep. Her mom wished she had done it years earlier. She was so amazed at simply how easy it was to do.

TROUBLESHOOTING

? *Why is it not a good idea for my child to fall asleep watching TV in their bedroom?*

It is not uncommon for households to have not just one or two TVs, but a TV and a DVD player in every bedroom. It could be a great temptation to leave your child to fall asleep in front of the TV, replacing yourself as a sleeping device with the TV. The difficulty with this is once your child wakes in the night they will need the TV on again to lull themselves back to sleep. The idea we are looking for here is to teach your child how to soothe themselves to sleep using no outside mechanism. There have also been studies that show that watching TV and playing computer games can decrease the amount of hours a child or adult sleeps (e.g. Cespedes *et al.* 2014; Thompson and Christakis 2005), concluding that if you reduce your child's screen time you may help increase their sleep time.

? *I live in an apartment building and I am concerned that if my child cries, the neighbors may be troubled.*

This may be a concern for many families living in blocks of flats/ apartments. One way round this that has worked well for a number of families I have worked with is either to write a letter or knock on the doors of the neighbors who may be affected and explain the situation—that you are helping your child with autism learn how to sleep through the night in their own bed, which means that they may cry for a couple of days, and that you would appreciate their support in this matter. Then you could bake them some cookies, or offer to help them with some task, inviting their co-operation and generosity. This communication often helps nourish others' understanding and kindness.

I am sure that some of you who read this suggestion may be thinking, "Ok, that is totally not me, I can't do something as forward as that." If you are one of those people, remember that you are doing this for your child. Remind yourself of all the benefits they will be getting by having a good night's sleep, and take the plunge. Sometimes we have to leave our habitual comfort zones and do daring action to get what we want. Or you might be surprised, as many parents are, that your child does not cry at length and this issue never arises! Or perhaps your child only cries for one night, which the neighbors have certainly already heard.

? *My child will fall asleep in her bed but will then come into my bed in the middle of the night. I do not mind, but should I stop her?*

This is your child and how you want to parent them is up to you; if you want her to sleep with you there is nothing wrong with this. One thing for you to consider is that our children can become very attached to routines. In my experience I have not heard of a child on the autism spectrum who magically decided that they wanted to sleep alone in their own bed. So consider the long-term outcome of having your child in your bed. How are they going to learn this if we do not teach it to them?

? *If I put my child to sleep at 7.30pm, she will wake up before 5am.*

This may be the case to begin with, but remember sleep begets sleep, the longer you leave your child in the morning the more likely your child will change their pattern and sleep through the night. If your child does wake up at 5am, do not go to them until 5.30am; then a week later do not go to them until 5.45am; and then the next week do not go to them until 6am, and so forth. By doing this you will be helping your child to extend the amount of time they sleep.

Teaching children to put themselves to sleep as described earlier in this chapter will help them put themselves to sleep again if they wake in the early hours of the morning.

Oftentimes parents will leave toys that their children like to entertain themselves with when they wake. I would not suggest this in the case of a child getting up too early. You do not want to give them any reason to get up and play. That does not mean that you cannot have some soft toys or books or magazines, just not electronic or otherwise more stimulating toys.

I would also suggest that you have blackout curtains in your child's room so that no sunlight gets in to wake your child. Also check for other sounds that might cause your child to wake, such as the heating or other systems clicking on at 5am.

SLEEPING ACTION CHECKLIST

☐ Get solid in your new bedtime mindset. See the bigger picture for your child—that sleeping regularly through the night will be of great benefit to them. It will help them focus, connect, and learn new things.

☐ Teach your child that bedtime is for sleeping, not for playing.

☐ Leave your child's room before they are actually asleep, thus creating the opportunity for them to learn to put themselves to sleep.

☐ Create a bedtime routine and stick to the same timeframe and actions.

☐ Explain to your child their new routine, and that if they call for you in the night you are here but will not be coming in and that you will see them in the morning.

☐ Give your child their new bedtime buddy.

☐ Check your child's diet and make sure that they are not eating foods that will keep them up rather than helping them sleep.

☐ Set the scene for bedtime an hour before. Only quiet, calm activities should be used during this time.

☐ Take your child back immediately if they leave their bedroom.

☐ Take your child back to their bed immediately if they come into your bed at night.

☐ Let your child cry without going into their bedroom. It will help them be able to put themselves back to sleep with your assistance.

I am so excited for your new bedtime plan! Go for it! Keep the big picture in mind. What you want for your child is to be able to sleep through the night in her own bed.

Chapter 11

SELF-HELP SKILLS

This chapter is dedicated to self-help skills, such as taking a bath, getting dressed, washing hair, brushing teeth, clipping nails, cutting hair, and learning to wear deodorant. I will talk about how we can make it easier for our children to allow us to do these things for them, and how to encourage our children to do these tasks for themselves.

When you think of attempting one of the above-mentioned activities, does it fill you with delight or dread? Is it something you want to get over as quickly as possible? If this is true for you, then the first place to start is with a change of attitude.

Sometimes we can view the self-help skills of self-grooming as a chore that has to be done, one to get over as quickly as possible so the "real" fun or the "real" learning can begin. This means that it is often done in a fast and unenjoyable way for our children. Seeing this time with our children as important and valuable will completely change the way you approach the activity, thus changing the way your child responds. The following perspectives may help you embrace its importance.

- **They are a step toward their independence.** The more our children take care of themselves, dress themselves, clean their own teeth, and take a bath, the more self-sufficient they become taking a great step toward their independence.

- **They will translate into you having more time.** The more our children can do things for themselves, the more time we will have to take care of the other things we want to do for our families and for ourselves.

- **They can help strengthen your relationship.** Whether we are changing our children's clothes, brushing their teeth,

199

or giving them a bath, we are interacting with them. This interaction is valuable. It is a time when we can show them our love, our tenderness, and the warmth of human interaction. It is a time when we show them that we can be trusted. A time to show them that we will listen. From these interactions we have a chance to understand their sensory challenges on a deeper level. Above all, it is a time to savor, rather than rushing through to the illusion of a better interaction or learning experience. We may spend an hour or more a day with our children in this way—if you are a working mom or dad, then this may be the only one-on-one time you spend with your children: getting them dressed in the morning, bathing them, and putting them to bed; let this time be a time that sets the tone of your relationship.

- **They will help our children become socially successful.** Self-grooming skills are just as helpful to a person's social life as any other skill they may learn. If our children allow us to cut their hair, it won't fall into their eyes and they will be more able to see the world and make eye contact with the people around them. If their nails are neatly cut, they will not accidently scratch someone as they reach out and play with their peers. If our children learn to have fun keeping themselves clean and presentable, they are more likely to develop a pride in their appearance and develop their own particular style and "look." All these can translate into a greater social ease.

- **They are fun activities for you and your child.** I would suggest that you do not label self-grooming skills as a task or chore. When we think of doing a chore, it is usually something we want to get over and done with as quickly as possible. Tasks and chores are usually associated with the interaction of objects, such as ironing, washing the kitchen floor, and mowing the lawn, rather than something we do that includes another person. So perhaps we can shift our perception to seeing the development of self-help skills with our child as an activity or game. Now we might think—A game? How can a self-grooming activity be a game? A game is something you do with another person, so how is this different? There are millions of different games. The common factor is that it is something that people enjoy and have fun engaging with.

THE SECRET INGREDIENTS TO YOUR SUCCESS
Make it fun! Be enthusiastic!

Fun is an essential ingredient to developing self-help skills. It is the secret weapon that will bring our children running to the bathroom with a smile on their faces. If we do not enjoy the activity we are asking our children to do, why should they?

Believing that the activity itself is important for your child will mean that we will want to take more care and time focusing on it. The second step is to believe that they can be fun and enjoyable for you! In order to inspire our children to want to do these activities we must make it fun and motivating for our children. We will be the most successful at that when we sincerely believe that the activity is fun. The way to do that is to believe that "fun" or "enjoyment" is in our attitude, not the activity itself.

People like to do different things—they like snooker, swimming, skiing, cooking, reading, movies, eating out, tango dancing, tap dancing, disco dancing, ice skating, rugby, running, working out, knitting, etc. Everyone likes different activities. If it were the actual game or the activity that made it fun and exciting then everybody would enjoy the same activities. Soccer might arguably be the most universal and widespread game enjoyed by people around the globe, but even that is not enjoyed by everyone. It is what the person actually decides to believe about the game that makes it fun and exciting for them. Maybe it was something the whole family played and it was the warmth of the whole family playing together that brought enjoyment to the game. Maybe it was the thrill of being celebrated for being good at a particular sport that added to the fun of the game. What we associate with the game can be more meaningful than the actual act of the game itself. *In short this means that we are in charge of how much fun we have at any given moment, with any activity.*

Transform the experience from dull to fun for yourself

EXERCISE 11.1
....

Take a self-grooming skill you do for yourself—any skill that you do not think is fun or enjoyable—and do the following things:

- **Get "in the moment."** When we do our own self-grooming activities we are often not in the moment. I am sure you will relate to thinking about your day while you are brushing your teeth so much that you hardly even notice the sensations of brushing your teeth. Next time you brush your teeth, or get yourself dressed, decide to pay attention to the activity at hand.

- **Enjoy one thing.** Now that you are being present with your own self-grooming activity, find one thing about a previously "boring" activity that you can get excited about. For instance, when you are brushing your teeth it might be the minty taste of your toothpaste. Or the way the toothbrush feels as it glides across your teeth. As you are getting dressed it may be the feel of the clothes on your skin. Or the perfect way the buttons fit into the button-holes as you do them up.

- **Remind yourself.** The next time you are about to do this activity for yourself, remind yourself of the one thing you like about it and begin to anticipate its delight. Actively build this excitement as you walk to the bathroom or other room in which the activity is to take place.

- **Slow down the activity.** When you do that particular part of the activity you like the most, slow it down and really savor it as if you are eating your favorite food.

- **Celebrate.** Once finished, praise yourself for doing a particularly great job. Celebrate out loud as you look in the mirror and admire the great job you just did.

- **Share the celebration.** Share what you enjoyed with a member of your family. Talking about what you enjoy makes it bigger.

....

The more you actively look for enjoyment the more likely you will find it. Enjoyment will build the more you decide to experience it, and when you talk about your enjoyment you confirm this to yourself. It's like watering seeds: when we water the seeds of enjoyment, it is enjoyment that grows. Your enjoyment is important because the more you enjoy an activity the more likely you will share this activity in a fun and inspiring way with your children.

Transform the experience from dull to fun for your child

Use your child's motivations. Make it fun for your child by marrying your child's existing motivations to the self-grooming goal you have for them. The more our children are motivated and enjoy an activity the easier it is for them to learn. So let's take what our children already really enjoy and these self-help skills and put them together. Remember, this is not about giving our child's motivation as a reward once the self-help skill is done, it is about putting your child's motivation at the center of the self-help skill. If you do not already know what your child is really motivated by, complete Exercise 4.1 (see Chapter 4), which will help you get a clear understanding of what your child likes. For example:

- If your child likes it when you talk in a funny voice, make funny voices as you/they brush their teeth.

- If they like the movie *Cars*, get a toothbrush with the car characters on it.

- If your child loves numbers, then count out loud or draw numbers for them as you/they brush their teeth.

- If your child loves to talk about the weather, pretend you're brushing your teeth in a thunderstorm or blizzard.

Often when our staff at the Autism Treatment Center of America teach a child to brush their teeth for the first time, or help a child successfully sit through nail clipping, the parents believe we have achieved a miracle! Really, what we have done is made the activity fun, fun, fun!

More fun ideas can be found in each of the self-grooming categories later in the chapter.

Be sensitive to your child's sensory experience

Anything that comes into contact with our children's bodies may be an overwhelming experience—an experience so unlike our own that it is hard for us to imagine. That is why it is so important not only to give a huge amount of control but also to really observe our children's responses carefully.

Even if our children are not overly sensitive to their surroundings, think of the usual things that are involved with self-grooming:

- strong-tasting toothpaste

- shampoo that stings the eyes

- hard toothbrushes that can slip and bruise the gums

- strong-smelling soaps, deodorants, and conditioners

- people doing things to our faces

- soaps that can dry out the skin

- hot and cold water

- rough bath towels and face flannels

- sounds of a hair buzzer, an electric razor, or hair dryers

- snap of the toenail clippers

- hard hair brushes with spiky teeth.

Our child's prior experience with one of the above may have been unpleasant enough for them to decide that they will not go near it again. Sometimes they may try to avoid the bathroom altogether. It may have been a time where they got soap in their eyes, the water was too hot, or a scratchy towel felt rough on their skin. Whatever it was, it was enough for them not to want to experience it again. What can we do to minimize this?

- Use unscented hypoallergenic products that do not smell.

- Make sure that the towels you use are fresh from the tumble dryer so that they are soft and fluffy, rather than rough or damp.

- Buy buzzers or razors that make the least amount of sound possible.

- Find toothpaste that tastes reasonable—not too sweet and not too sharp.

- Test the water yourself, then dab a little on your child's hand or foot, and either watch their reaction to it or ask them how it feels before they step into the bathtub.

- Go into your bathroom and look around from a sensory perspective.

  ○ Does your bathroom have a particular smell, either mildew or over-perfumed from toilet cleaners, air fresheners, and other cosmetics? Find the culprit and get rid of it. Exchange anything you throw out for unscented products.

  ○ Does your bathroom have a particular sound that may be overwhelming for your child? Maybe a loud fan or hot water system? Does your bathtub make a loud echoed sound when a bottle of shampoo falls into it? Find out if there is anything you can do to minimize these sounds.

  ○ How is the lighting in your bathroom? If it is fluorescent, it may be particularly challenging for your child. Consider changing to incandescent lighting, which unlike fluorescent lighting does not flicker or produce a hum.

EXERCISE 11.2

Before you start working on a self-grooming skill with your child, take the time to observe your child interacting with all the toiletries you use. Notice if they move more toward some rather than others. Notice which ones they seem to avoid.

If your child is highly verbal ask them about their experience; you could ask them all or some of the following questions:

- Why do you like this toothpaste?

- Why do you not like this toothpaste?

- Why do you not want to take a bath or a shower?

- How does the shower feel on your skin?

- Do you like the smell of this shampoo?
- What kind of sounds do you hear in the bathroom?
- Why will you only wear "X" piece of clothing?

With this knowledge you can make the experience easier on your child's sensory system.

....

Take the fight out of the equation: Give control

If our children are to become open to engaging with self-grooming activities, they must feel that they are in control of the situation. It must be something that they can direct and accomplish at their own pace, not something that is thrust upon them with no warning.

If you have held your child down to brush their teeth, or forced them to cut or wash their hair, they most likely will associate these activities with being held down, and with the struggle and lack of control that ensues. You might believe that your child is frightened of the toothbrush or nail clippers as they start to cry or run and hide when they see them, not understanding that it is the struggle of being held down that they are running from rather than the activity itself (see Chapter 1).

You may have got into the habit of holding your child down because it is just easier to get the job done and then you can move on to something else. If you want your child to love brushing their own teeth and allow you to easily brush their hair, then I would recommend that you stop holding them down or forcing these activities upon them as soon as possible. The idea is that we want to inspire our children to want to brush their own teeth, or to love getting their hair cut and getting dressed. This is possible by putting into practice the following strategies.

The Control Protocol

How to do this is detailed in Chapter 1. If you have not yet read about "giving control" in Chapter 1, I would highly recommend that you do this before putting the Control Protocol into practice, as this will give you a deeper understanding of the protocol itself. You can also see a video demonstration of the Control Protocol on YouTube (see www.youtube.com/watch?v=yuGlgjm23EE).

- Use this protocol every time you do a self-grooming activity with your child. This will ensure that you give them a sense of control, and thus greatly increase your child's openness to doing the activity.

- Using the Control Protocol, you would take the following steps:

    1. Make sure your child can see you.

    2. Tell them what you are doing.

    3. Look for permission.

    4. Stop if they indicate or say "No."

Below is an example of how to implement this protocol with the self-help skill of brushing teeth.

1. Position yourself in front of your child with the toothbrush in your hand so that they can see what you are going to do.

2. Explain to them verbally what you are about to do. You could say something like "I am going to brush your teeth so that we can make them nice and clean and keep them healthy and strong. Open your mouth so that we can brush those lovely teeth."

3. Slowly bring the toothbrush up to their mouth. As you do that, look for their permission to proceed. If they either open their mouth, say "Yes," or show no signs that they do not want you to brush their teeth, go ahead and gently brush their teeth.

4. If they say "No" or indicate no by moving away or pushing the toothbrush away, stop. It is very important that our children feel that we will listen to their "Nos."

The Control Protocol works! Giving our children control and respecting their "Nos" helps them to become flexible and open to activities they had previously resisted. This is true for every child I have worked with, without exception. However, it does not mean that it happens overnight. Once we give our children control in this way they may want to test us, to see if we really mean it. Even if they say or indicate no for a few weeks, we will still stop and not force them. Stay the distance. Once your child really believes that you will not force them anymore, they will begin to open up and try because they trust that you will stop if they say no.

Make friends with the activity

This applies to all self-help skills, such as hair brushing, taking a bath, cutting finger and toe nails, brushing teeth, hair cutting, wearing deodorant, and getting dressed. Do this by letting them explore these objects without the threat of them being used on them. For example, put a few toothbrushes around the house where your child can reach them. When you are engaging with your child, perhaps tickling or playing, you can pick up a toothbrush and tickle them with it. If your child is engaging with a soft toy or a character, pretend that you are cleaning the character's or soft toy's teeth. This way your child begins to associate the object with something pleasurable and fun, and may begin to move toward rather than away from it. See each self-grooming category below for ideas on how to do this.

TOOTHBRUSHING
Concerned for your children's teeth?

Giving your children control over whether you brush their teeth or not may sound unreasonable to you. You may think that if you give your child control in this area they will just never clean their teeth again, and then they will get cavities and that is another ordeal all by itself. If you want your child to clean their teeth easily without you forcing them, then giving control is the only way to go. There is just no other way around it. Your child has to feel that they can control what is happening in order to open up to the teeth-cleaning experience. Once they know that their "Yes" or "No" will be respected then they may dare to explore an experience that may have been painful for them.

The way to do this is for you to let go! Let go of them having clean teeth for this present moment, and hold on to the dream of your child making friends with the toothbrush and cleaning their teeth without a fuss. Giving control is a very clear technique that will help pave the way for your child to let go of any resistance they may have and to become open to new experiences. Once they are more open, you will have the highest chance of your child not only allowing you to brush their teeth but also brushing their teeth themselves.

Control coupled with fun, delight, and persistence will win in the long term over pressure and force.

For those of you who are not quite sure, could you give your child control over cleaning their teeth for just two weeks? This would mean that for two weeks, whenever your child says or indicates "No" to you brushing their teeth, you stop. You stop "pushing" your child to clean their teeth. During those two weeks you focus instead on making brushing teeth a fun and motivating activity for your child. You drop the "forcing" but you pick up the idea of helping your child, "make friends with the toothbrush," using the concepts and the ideas listed below. At the end of two weeks, if you are still not convinced that this is the way to go, you can go back to your old system. You have nothing to lose and a lot to gain. Read to the end of the toothbrushing section and then decide.

During this two-week period there is a lot you can do to help clean your children's teeth other than brushing. Make sure that they drink lots of water to help clean out their mouth. Have them munch on apples that help clean the plaque on their teeth. Feed your children healthy foods and lay off soda and sugar, major culprits in helping rot your children's teeth.

Be gentle

For those of you who brush your child's teeth yourself, be aware that it can be a very painful experience. If you are rough or slip by accident and the toothbrush bangs into their gums, it hurts big time, and it could be this pain that your child is moving away from. If you have held your child down and forced a toothbrush into their mouths, this has most likely happened many times.

Model toothbrushing

It is important to show or model toothbrushing and how fun it can be! Have the whole family brush their teeth in a dramatic way. Just before you want your child to brush their teeth, have the whole family declare that they are going to brush their teeth. Then all of you go into the bathroom at the same time and brush your teeth in a synchronized fashion to the beat of your child's favorite song. Put out your child's toothbrush and toothpaste within easy reach just in case your child wants to join in. Don't feel that you have to force your child to watch this event. If you do it in an obvious way, making sure that the TV or the computer is off in the house, your child will know that it is going on. Try this at least every day for a two-week period. Of course, you don't have to do it in the same way each time. You can get creative in your own way.

Ideas for making friends with the toothbrush

The ideas listed below are designed to help your child get comfortable with the toothbrush and toothpaste, as well as with the actual action of brushing your teeth *without it happening to them*. That way they can engage in the activity without the need to protect themselves against the brushing. Our first intention is to simply get our child to enjoy the toothbrush. At the beginning it is important not to ask or attempt to brush your children's teeth. We are just playing and exploring. If they sense you are about to brush their teeth they will most likely move away from the experience. Once they have relaxed and are enjoying playing with the toothbrush we can start to ask them to brush their own teeth or have us brush their teeth. We want our children to feel no "push" or "pressure" from us to actually clean their teeth.

The games below are also an inspiration for you. Use them as a springboard to design games that you think your child will be motivated for. Each game builds from you doing something with the toothbrush to your child actually engaging with the toothbrush. In each game, Part 1 is just you doing something fun with the toothbrush; Part 2 is about encouraging your child to interact with the toothbrush.

Spelling game

Part 1. You spell out different words with the toothbrushes.

Part 2. You ask your child to spell out a letter or word using toothbrushes.

Microphone game

Part 1. You hold a toothbrush under your chin like a microphone. You can hold one under your child's chin as they sing too.

Part 2. Ask your child to hold a toothbrush under his or your own chin as you sing their favorite song.

Drum game

Part 1. You bang and tap rhythms with the toothbrushes: take two toothbrushes and bang out interesting rhythms on different surfaces.

Part 2. Ask your child to hold the toothbrush and bang it also.

Treasure hunt game

Part 1. You create a treasure hunt for your child where each clue is taped to toothbrushes hidden around the room.

Part 2. Ask them to create a toothbrush treasure hunt for you.

Story game

Part 1. Write a story about the case of the missing toothbrush, where your child's favorite character is the detective who solves the mystery.

Part 2. Ask your child to act this out; have your child find the toothbrush and bring it to you.

Joke game

Part 1. You take two toothbrushes and pretend that they are two people telling each other silly jokes.

Part 2. Ask your child to be the puppeteer of one of the toothbrushes.

Gift game

Part 1. You decorate a toothbrush with stickers, and give to Grandma as a gift.

Part 2. Ask your child to decorate a toothbrush and give it as a gift.

Character game

Part 1. You make different characters talk about their favorite toothbrush. Maybe Buzz Lightyear's is red with moon and stars on it, and Dora the Explorer's has a backpack. You can draw each character's toothbrush.

Part 2. Ask your child to draw the patterns the characters like on actual toothbrushes.

Create your own design game

Part 1. You design your own toothbrush.

Part 2. Ask your child to design their own toothbrush.

Soft toy game

Part 1. You line up all their soft toys and brush their teeth and put them to bed.

Part 2. Ask your child to brush one of the soft toy's teeth.

Singing game

Part 1. You make up a song with actions. Have one of the actions be brushing your teeth. When you get to that part of the song, put toothpaste on a toothbrush and actually brush your teeth.

Part 2. Ask your child to do the actions of the song too.

Race game

Part 1. Get some wind-up "chatter teeth." Wind them up on a small table and try to brush their teeth before they fall off the table.

Part 2. Invite your child to try to do the same.

Persist

While you are modeling toothbrushing and helping your child make friends with the process, do still ask your child to brush their own teeth or offer to brush them for them each morning and night. As you offer:

- **Be excited.** This could be the first time that your child willingly lets you clean their teeth without resistance. Or maybe it will be the first time that they hold the toothbrush and put it in their mouth.

- **If they say or indicate no, then give them control.** Highlight in a big way that you are giving them control. You might say, "Thank you so much for telling me 'no,' you will not brush your teeth." Make a big "happy" show of putting the toothbrush away. Let them know that you are happy to give them control in this way. This will clearly give the message to your child that we are listening to them and give them a heightened sense of control. Remember, the more control we give the less controlling our children will become.

GETTING DRESSED
Allow plenty of time

Successfully getting your child dressed in the morning is about allocating a longer period of time than usual to the process. This will mean that you do not feel rushed and pressured, thus alleviating your child of your pressure.

For your morning routine leave at least one hour to get your child ready for school. That would include dressing, toothbrushing, and breakfast. Feeling relaxed that there is plenty of time will help you approach this skill with ease and give your child the necessary control.

Do as much as you can the night before so that you have more time to help your child get dressed. Packing their school lunch and school bag, as well as setting the breakfast table, will save so much time and give you the time to focus on and interact with your child.

Get them dressed first

This is such a small change but can yield amazing results. I was consulting via Skype with the parents of a six-year-old boy called Ali. One of the first areas they wanted help with was how to help their child get dressed in time for the school bus. Unable to get him dressed in time, they had on many occasions either missed the school bus altogether or sent him to school with his pajamas on. They wanted to know how to accomplish this at the same time as giving him control.

What was happening was that every time they asked him to put on an item of clothing he would say, "Yes, I will do that, but you have to sing a song to me first." Once they had sung the song he would invent another thing that they had to do, such as pretend to be an airplane and fly him around the room. This could go on and on and on. They both felt that they were being controlled by him, and wanted to know how to shift this dynamic.

I asked them about his morning routine. They would get him up and he would play with his toys while they made him breakfast; then he would eat breakfast and get to play again; and then they would go and try and get him dressed for school. I asked if he was hungry and motivated to eat and play with his toys. They said he was. The solution we evolved was just to change the order of his routine. I suggested that they get him dressed before he ate breakfast or played with his toys. I suggested that they explain this change in his routine to him the night before they began it.

The first morning that this new routine was in place they stayed true to what they had said and every time he asked for his breakfast they said, "Yes, I will get you that as soon as you are dressed." When he asked to play with his toys, they said, "Yes, you can play with your toys as soon as you are dressed." They had put his toys away out of reach until he was dressed so that he could not just help himself to them.

The second time I consulted with them, I asked how the new strategy went. They said it was unbelievable—he took to it straight away and it only took one day to implement—and now he gets dressed easily every day. Also he dresses himself instead of making them dress him. One simple change transformed their morning from stressed to easy.

Create a rule that your child needs to be dressed and washed before they do anything else in the morning. That means that your child will get dressed before breakfast and before any TV or computer time. This will encourage your child to get on with the process of dressing, especially if they are motivated by another activity that they can only do after they are dressed. Doing it in this way may even give your child some time to play after they have dressed, washed, and eaten, thus transforming a previously stressed morning.

In order to make this happen make sure that the TV and the computer are unplugged and not accessible to your child until they have dressed and eaten. If your child has already left their bedroom in the morning, take their clothes to wherever they are and explain to them that they can watch the TV or have breakfast once they are dressed. Set your boundary lovingly but firmly (see Chapter 2), and they will soon get familiar with the new morning routine.

Put your child's clothes out the night before

Another useful strategy is to put your child's clothes out the night before. Show these clothes to your child so that they know in advance what they will be wearing. If you have a highly verbal child, you can include them in the decision-making process. Giving them this choice may result in them being more motivated and flexible to wear them the next day.

Making it happen

Just ask your child

If your child is fine with you dressing them and you want to encourage them to dress themselves, just ask. Start with little steps and build up to the big things such as zippers and buttons.

While you are teaching your child to dress themselves make sure you start with easy-to-handle clothes such as sweat pants and shirts without buttons. Start with little steps such as the following:

- Help them step into their underwear and ask your child to pull them up. If they try a little, celebrate their effort and do the rest. Next time ask them to do a little more; keep challenging them until they are able to get them all the way up. Do the same with their trousers/pants.

- Hold out the trouser legs and ask them to step into them. Do the same with their shirt and sweater, showing them where to put their hands. If you start the morning earlier, thus allowing yourself more time, you will have the time to help your child learn to take a bigger role in dressing themselves. They then get to learn a new skill and you get even more time in the morning!

• Once they have mastered the above steps, give them a pair of trousers or a shirt and ask them to put it on themselves. If they are having trouble, help them by putting on a pair of trousers or shirt yourself so that they can copy how you do it.

Be fun and playful!

Be fun and playful as you ask your child to get dressed. For example, when asking your child to step into his trouser leg:

• You could sing instead of just asking.

• You could add a little imagination and pretend that the trouser hole is a puddle and ask them to step into the "trouser puddle." When they put their foot in, you could say, "Splash."

• You could pretend that the trousers are asking. You could pretend the trousers, mouth is the top opening of the trousers and have them say in a silly trouser voice, "I want someone to wear me. Will someone please put their foot into me? Oh I see a lovely child here—will you wear me?"

As you bring the trousers over to them you could playfully wave them in the air, making them do a trouser dance. Try making a fun sound when you do the buttons or a zipper on your child's clothing. You could make a "clicking" noise as the buttons fit into their holes. You could make a "zoom" sound as you do the zipper up. As they put their arm into their jumper/sweater you could make a "whoosh" sound. Not only might your child find these sounds funny or interesting, but it also brings an added sense of fun and delight to the dressing process for you and your child.

Model getting dressed!

Have your child watch you get dressed. As you get dressed show them how much fun you are having putting your clothes on. You could say out loud things like, "Oh, it feels so nice and warm to have my sweater on." Or you could explain how you put on the sweater by saying something like, "Ok, first I have to find the holes for the arms... Ok, great, that's arm number one. Now let's find arm hole number two..." By doing this you are verbally walking them through the process you take to get dressed. In the morning you could take your clothes into your child's room and get dressed together.

Celebrate! Celebrate! Celebrate!

Celebrate everything your child does in relation to them putting on their clothes. Praise them:

- when they look at their clothes

- for touching their clothes

- for any attempt they make to put their clothes on

- when they let you put any piece of clothing on them.

Troubleshooting getting dressed

? *My child will wear clothes at school but will not wear clothes at home.*

This is usually an indication that your child may be very sensitive to the way the clothes feel on their skin—meaning that the different textures of their clothing may feel very uncomfortable. They may be able to tolerate clothes enough to go outside where they are aware enough to know they have to wear clothes, but once within the safety of their home they will take their clothes off as soon and as often as possible.

The following suggestions will help with the underlying reason why they are not wearing clothes.

- Consider using the Wilbarger Deep Pressure and Proprioceptive Technique. This protocol, created by occupational therapist and clinical psychologist Patricia Wilbarger, is a specific, professionally guided treatment regime designed to reduce sensory defensiveness. It involves deep-touch pressure throughout the day. I have seen this to be very useful for a number of children I have worked with and is something you can implement with your child at home (for more information on the technique, see www.ot-innovations.com/content/view/55/46).

- Observe how your child interacts with different materials—is there one material they gravitate toward? If there is, find clothes in this material. Buy clothes that are soft and made with one texture only. Stay away from clothes that have a ribbed or bumpy texture in their patterns, buttons, zips, sequins, rhinestones, or plastic pictures ironed onto the material. Take all labels off. Any change in the texture of the clothing may be an irritant for your child. Clothing that is 100 percent cotton is often the best option.

- Wash your child's clothes in unscented hypoallergenic detergent. Some washing detergents can leave a strong scent on the clothes that may be overpowering for a child who has an overactive sense of smell.

The suggestions below will help to motivate your child to want to wear clothes.

- Sometimes when children take their clothes off we accommodate this by putting up the heating. I would suggest that you do the opposite: and open a window—put the heating down, give your child a reason to put on their clothes. Explain to them that putting clothes on would warm them up. Model this by saying, "Oh, I feel a little chilly," and then put on a jumper.

- Praise them every time they do wear clothes, letting them know how handsome and beautiful they look fully dressed.

- If they are naked and they want something from you, either a snack or toy that they cannot reach by themselves, or maybe they want to play chase or have a piggyback ride, this is the time to ask them to put their clothes on. We are more likely to do the things that are hard for us when we want something. Below is an outline of how to ask your child to get dressed using the example of your naked child having asked you for a snack:

  ○ Say "Yes, I would love to get you a snack."

  ○ More toward the kitchen.

- ○ Stop before you get the snack and say a version of, "Oh, you are naked—let's get dressed before you eat your snack. The snack is sticky and your body will get dirty [or the snack is hot and it might burn your body]. That's why we wear clothes to protect our skin."

- ○ The idea here is to think up a reason why it is important for your child to put their clothes on. This way we are communicating to them that we are helping them by asking them to put their clothes on.

- ○ Be persistent with asking them; bring their clothes to them and help them put them on. As you continue to ask them, keep telling them that you will get them a snack once their clothes are on.

- ○ You don't have to get them fully dressed; begin with just putting on either a T-shirt or trousers and gradually work up from there.

- ○ It is very important to get them the snack or whatever they were asking for as soon as they put on the item of clothing.

- ○ It is ok if they take their clothes off as soon they get the snack—the idea is to give them as many experiences of wearing clothes as possible. The more they wear them, the more they will get used to the feeling on their skin.

It is important to feel easy and relaxed when your child is not wearing clothes. If we get uptight and uncomfortable, our child will pick up on this and push against our need for him to wear clothes. Thoughts that will help you feel relaxed when your child is not wearing clothes:

- • It is ok that my child is not wearing clothes. They are doing this for a reason, and I know some steps to take to help my child wear clothes.

- • Encouraging my child to wear clothes is a process; it does not have to happen right this minute.

- • The more calm and accepting I feel, the more opportunities I will create to help my child wear clothes.

? *My child has challenges changing into different clothes for different seasons. We have a battle every change of season.*

Our children can get very attached to routine, becoming inflexible when it is time for a transition or change. It is most likely that your child is protesting against change. To help your child make the transition easily do it as a gradual process. For example, during the summer months have your child wear some light shirts and jackets with long sleeves, and full-length trousers. That way it won't be so alien to your child when the summer ends and you ask them to wear autumn/winter tops and trousers. As the summer ends have them wear these tops more often and gradually swop them for progressively heavier material. You can do the reverse in the winter months. This way it is not so much of an immediate change for your child.

? *My child will not wear his winter coat.*

This may simply be due to the fabric of their coat. Most winter coats can be "puffy" and have a plastic feel; others can be very heavy, and may feel a little suffocating due to the coat going right up to your child's chin.

Experiment with different coats; I would suggest that you start with the softest, most lightweight fabric you can find and do not do it all the way up. This may help your child tolerate the feel of it more.

Make wearing a coat fun. Weave wearing a coat into the everyday games you play with your child. You could do the following:

- While playing a chase game with your child, grab your child's coat and wrap him in it, giving him a squeeze once you catch him.

- Next time you play a "going to sleep" game with your child, have his coat be the comforter.

- Try wearing his coat and have him wear your coat.

- Put the coat on his favorite characters or soft animals and take pictures of them in silly positions.

- Make a tent out of your coats and invite your child to play with you inside.

- If you and your child play imagination games together, like going on an airplane, catching a train, or going to the moon, add putting your coat on as part of the game.

- Hide little things you know your child will find interesting inside his coat pockets. Maybe it is a sticker, a picture of his favorite character, a snack he likes, or pieces of string or a balloon.

Remember to talk to your child and really explain why you are asking him to wear his coat—how it will help him keep warm and dry.

? *At times my child is so absorbed in his own activity that it is hard to get him away from it so that I can get him dressed.*

Go with, rather than against, the activity your child is engrossed in. When you move with your child's interest they will more likely allow you to dress them. In this case there is no need to move your child's attention away from his activity. You can simply get him dressed where he is. Let's say your child is standing at the table absorbed in a Thomas the Tank Engine book—dress them as they are standing. Use the Control Protocol (see Chapter 1) and let them know they can still look at the book while you get them dressed.

BATHTIME

Yeah! It's bathtime! Images of bubble bath and little yellow ducks come to mind. Bathtime is traditionally at the end of the day. This can be useful as it washes off the dirt collected from the day and can have a calming effect on our children, which helps soothe them for sleep. You, on the other hand, may feel tired and a little stressed from a full day. If you sometimes feel too tired to face giving your children a bath, there are a couple of options for you:

- If you have flexibility, you could pick a time of day that suits you better. Maybe it would be more relaxed and easy for you to bath your children in the morning, or even midday. The choice is yours.

- If you do not have that flexibility, with nighttime being the only feasible time to bath your child, then it would be important for you to bring a relaxed, fun energy to it. This brings us back to the notion that it not the activity itself that is fun or not fun. We bring our own delight and fun to each activity. Keep this in mind as bathtime approaches and find something about it to enjoy. As it nears—relax and embrace that it's bathtime! You are going to do it anyway, so you might as well do it with a sense of relaxation and enjoyment.

Having trouble getting your child into the bathtub?
Give them a decent warning

Give your child enough notice that bathtime is imminent. Sometimes our children are too absorbed in their current activity and do not want to suddenly leave it to take a bath. Let them know 15 minutes ahead of time that bathtime will be soon. Then give them a ten-minute warning and after that a five-minute warning, so that it will not be such a surprise when the actual bathtime comes.

Similarly, if you know you want to get your child in the bathtub in 30 minutes' time, do not introduce an activity for your child that is challenging to move him on from. I would suggest that you put all electronics away and do not start a big puzzle or another similar activity that your child may want to finish completely before moving on.

Check out any sensory sensitivity

As with the previous section on wearing clothes, reluctance to get into the bath could be due to a sensory sensitivity. The sound of the running water hitting the sides of the bath could be too intense. One suggestion would be to run the bath before you have your child come into the bathroom. Experiment with the opposite: have your child get into an empty bath and then fill it up. This is especially effective if your child likes to watch water.

It may be the temperature of the water that is bothersome to your child; experiment with offering a colder or a warmer bath.

A lot of children I have worked with enjoy being in really small places. If your child is small enough you can wash them in the sink, or in a smaller basin or tub inside the bathtub. Consider different forms of washing, such as a shower.

Let them bring their ism/stim toy

If your child has a special item or toy they like to hold or ism/stim with and it is either waterproof or would not be damaged by the water, let them play with it in the bath. This may help them want to get in the tub and become beautifully clean. You are the one who wants your child to take a bath. Why should they go if they have to leave their favorite and most important item behind? Our children have an ism toy for a reason. It is calming, and helping them get through their day in a world that is chaotic and unpredictable. Instead of thinking of it as getting in their way of taking a bath, see it as something that will help them take a bath. If you let them bring it with them, chances are they will move more easily to the bathroom and into the bath.

Make it fun!

- There are so many bathtub toys on the market right now you are really spoilt for choice. Remember to marry your child's motivation with any bathtub toy you buy (see chapter 4).

- Bubbles! Bubbles! Bubbles!—so often a great motivator for our children. I am not just talking about bubble bath, which would be a great idea, but you blowing bubbles into the bathtub once your child has hopped in. Bathtime could be your special and only time of day when the bubbles come out to play.

- Play your child's favorite music in the background.

- You could have the bath by candlelight or with a nightlight. This would make a super calming environment.

- You could buy a "bath friend." It could be a large plastic doll, blow-up animal, or character that comes out only at bathtime to take a bath with your child.

- You could use this "bath friend" to model getting into the bath when you ask.

HAIR WASHING

Hair washing can be particularly challenging for our children for numerous reasons. Our children can be particularly sensitive to different kinds of touch on their head and scalp, making the sensation of water being poured on their head unpleasant. The surprise of the water being poured on their head from a place they cannot see may give them a feeling of being out of control; thus their refusal to have their hair washed is an effort to reclaim control over the situation. Previous experiences of getting soap in their eyes may have put them off the whole experience.

Let go of the need for your child to have their hair washed

What harm can come of this? So your child has dirty hair for a while. This is not the end of the world. The oils that will be produced by not washing their hair will be nourishing and healthy for their hair and scalp. As a society we can over-wash our hair, eliminating all the natural oils that are there for a reason. The benefit of doing this will outweigh a few days of dirty hair. Giving your child the chance to gain control over this experience will, by not washing their hair if they say or indicate no, open them up to exploring and making friends with having their hair washed.

I worked with Millie, a young girl of four who refused to have her hair washed. Wanting to give her control, we kept offering to wash her hair in different and creative ways; but if she indicated or said no, we respected that and did not push or force her. She refused to let us wash her hair for three weeks. Those three weeks reaped big rewards in two ways. We were dedicated to giving her control, knowing that this was the most useful thing we could do—knowing that respecting her "No" was building a deep trust between us. This meant that we had to be more creative in how we went about washing her hair. This ultimately led us to the idea of putting a mirror in front of her so that she could see the water falling on her head, taking away the surprise. This helped her accept hair washing. Giving her this control not only led to her allowing us to wash her hair, but also built such a strong sense of trust between her and her parents that she started to allow them to do other things. Today she is a teenager who takes great pride in making her hair look good.

Get creative

Try different ways to wash your child's hair:

- Try using a mirror as in the story above.

- You could wet their hair by having them lie down in the bathtub. This again gives your child more control.

- You could use a jug and have your child watch the water being poured over a doll's hair first and then attempt to pour it over their head.

- Bring any plastic dolls you have into the bath and wash their hair, and then ask your child to participate in washing the doll's hair.

- Have your special child and their sibling take a bath together; wash their sibling's hair and have him express delight in the process before you wash your child's hair.

- Talk through a favorite puppet or figurine; have that figurine ask your child to wash their hair. I have seen children be more open to responding to requests when they are made through a puppet versus a person. I believe that this is because it is one step away from purely interacting with a person, making it easier for your child to respond.

- Pour the shampoo into your child's hand and have them massage it as best they can into their own hair. This would give them complete control over the process.

Desensitize their head

During the day and at playtime when your child is engaging with you, offer strong squeezes to their head. Massage the head using deep pressure. You could also scratch their scalp if they allow it. This will help to desensitize your child to having their head touched. Of course, as always, use the Control Protocol (see Chapter 1).

HAIR CUTTING

We all have a vision of the way we want our children's hair to look. There is nothing wrong with this, but sometimes somewhere along the line we may have put hair cutting into the category of a health necessity. Is it really? If your child is refusing to have their hair cut ask yourself if it is necessary. Can you put aside your desire to have your girl with a cute haircut or your boy to have the more traditional short hair? Nowadays it seems that every style is accepted. I see boys with really long hair (my 14-year-old nephew has hair nearly reaching his bottom), shaved heads, and Mohawks; I see girls with traditional bobs, short pixie cuts, and long locks. If you can put aside your ideal vision of how you would like your child's hair to be, in favor of giving your child control, it will decrease the amount of stress you both experience. This is something that you can let go of.

The benefit of your child being willing to have their hair cut will mean that it will be less likely to fall into or cover their eyes. This will make it easier for them to look at and communicate with the people around them. You may be able to keep it in a style that is easy to manage, keep clean, and look nice, which may help them look more appealing to their peers. Giving control by respecting our child's "No" now is the path to helping them move toward being willing to have their hair cut in the future.

Make friends with the process

While you let go of cutting your child's hair, encourage your child to make friends with the process. Below are some fun game suggestions:

- Line up some old Barbies and soft toys, and play hairdressers. If your child does not interact in imagination games yet, do this activity yourself while they are in the room. It does not matter if they show no signs of being interested in what you are doing. Remember to have fun and enjoy playing, and trust that your child will notice your enjoyment.

- If your child can interact in imagination games, play hairdressers and include your child in the game. Remember that it is not about cutting your child's hair, it is to help your child become comfortable with the process. Have them pretend to be the hairdresser as well as the customer.

- If your child likes play dough, make a man with long hair and cut his hair.

- Model cutting a family member's hair in front of your child.

I worked with one family who had a six-year-old boy called Billy who would scream and run away any time a pair of scissors appeared, worried that he would be held down and forced to have his hair cut. At that time we had Suzanne, a Son-Rise Program child facilitator, on staff who was also a hairdresser. To demonstrate to his parents how to make the process of having a haircut fun, while giving Billy complete control, Suzanne and I went into the playroom with Billy. Billy went into the playroom happily with us. When Suzanne got out her black hairdressing cape and began to explain to Billy that he was going to help cut my hair, he looked a little quizzical. When she produced her hair-cutting scissors he ran into the bathroom and closed the door. We gave Billy complete control, letting him stay in the bathroom alone for as long as he needed. While he was in the bathroom, we made sure we made plenty of fun noises about having my hair cut. We "aahed," we laughed, and we "oohed," talking out loud about how wonderful having your hair cut was, and most importantly we were sincerely having a good time.

About ten minutes into the haircut he opened the door less than an inch and looked through. When we turned to look at him he closed it immediately. We carried on, not asking him to do anything. Two minutes later he peeked in again; this time we knew better, so we did not look over at him—we just let him watch. He watched for at least a minute, and then closed the door. Once he trusted that we would not make him do anything and that it was not his turn to have his hair cut, he got braver and braver and actually came into the playroom to watch, and helped Suzanne to cut my hair by actually holding the scissors with her.

This was the first time he had voluntarily been in the same room as a pair of scissors, held a pair of scissors, and relaxed enough to laugh and have a good time. This took just 45 minutes, and shows how powerful the combination of giving control and making things fun can be.

Once your child has made friends with the process and is relaxed, start to ask if you can cut their hair.

- Begin with just one little snip.

- Praise them if they allow you.

- Wait a few days and see if you can cut two little snips.

- Work up from there, cutting more as time goes on.

- Once your child is comfortable with you cutting their hair, progress to a hairdresser.

If they refuse to let you cut their hair, give control and know that your child needs more time getting comfortable with the hair-cutting process. Try again in a couple of days. Keep going with the process; have persistence and an attitude of letting go. It is most likely that in their own time your child will manage a haircut and maybe even allow you to take them to a hairdresser.

Having your child's hair cut at a salon

I would make sure that your child is completely comfortable and easy with you cutting their hair for at least two months before even considering taking them to a salon. When that day arrives and you think it is time to progress to an actual hair salon first explain the whole process to your child. Maybe first go to the hair salon and take pictures so that you can show them to your child while you explain in detail what is going to happen. Remember to share this with great excitement that they are lucky that they are all grown up and ready to have their hair cut in a real salon. As well as explaining, you can act it out together. Pretend to get in the car and drive to the salon. Pretend that you are the hairdresser and greet your child; get them into a cape and sit them in the special hair-cutting chair. Pretend to wash their hair and cut and dry it. You could even ask the salon if they are willing for your child to come in afterhours to explore the salon. That way they have a chance to get familiar and make friends with the place where they are going to have their hair cut without the stress of actually having their hair cut.

If you find that the smells and the lights of a salon are just too much for your child, ask if one of the hairdressers will come to the house to cut your child's hair. You have nothing to lose by asking.

NAIL CUTTING

Nail cutting is the same process; give control and make friends with the process. It will also be extremely useful to explain and demonstrate to your child how the nail clipper works.

Making friends with the nail clippers

Below are some creative ideas, but don't forget, you can modify them to include your own child's motivations (see chapter 4).

- Pretend that the nail clippers are animals. One could be a shark, an alligator, or a caterpillar. Make paper fruit or fish and have the animal nail clippers eat the fruit.

- You could pretend that they are trains or airplanes. Have the pretend nail clipper vehicles travel to nail clipper land where all the Disney characters go to have their nails clipped.

- Bang the drums with nail clippers instead of drum sticks.

- Print out your child's favorite characters from the Internet and clip their nails.

- Make paper handprints of all the family and have your child clip their fingernails.

Once you feel that your child is relaxed with the nail clippers and fully understands the process, begin to try and clip their nails. Start with the hand, as it is easier for your child to see what is going on. Again, start with one clip and build up to doing the whole hand or foot.

Try clipping their nails when they are in the bathtub. The heat and the water make the nails softer, which might make it an easier sensory experience for your child.

ADOLESCENT HYGIENE

This section is for teenagers and young adults who are high functioning, meaning that they can hold a conversation, ask and answer questions, and read and write to some degree. It tackles the self-grooming skills of wearing deodorant, changing clothes, cleansing their adolescent skin, and brushing their hair. I will address these skills as a group versus individually.

Everything I talked about previously in this chapter will be relevant for your teenager or young adult; the process of giving control and making friends with the process is relevant for each of the above self-grooming skills. The difference here will be taking into consideration their age and stage in life.

Talk to your child

Talk to your child about their body and the changes that are occurring. All adolescents have concerns about their developing bodies; just because your child is on the autism spectrum does not shield them or make them immune. They will most likely have felt the changes going on in their bodies and have thoughts and feelings about them. That is why it is essential to give them clear and useful information about what is happening to their bodies. Then we know we have done our best to help them make sense of what is happening. I would suggest that you do this in two ways.

First, give them books that have been written in a clear and open way about how their body changes. Read and discuss these books with them, answer their questions, and bring up any questions that they may have but have not asked. Try your best to do this in the most open way; the more your child has real information about what is happening, the more likely they will be at ease with what is happening.

Second, be excited and delighted when discussing the changes that they are going through. So often our children are told this information in a tight and uncomfortable way, adding to or creating a lack of openness and comfort in our children's view of their own bodies. The more relaxed we are, the more likely our children will be relaxed. If you are in a family situation where the father can talk to the son and the mother can talk to the daughter, that would be ideal. Adolescents are often more willing to hear this type of information from a same-sex adult. If however you are a single parent, your openness and comfort will be enough. I encourage each of you to be the person who talks to your child; do not leave it up to the school or caring professional, as no one can care for your child as much as you. This way you also get to pass on your own values to your child.

Explain the whys behind the new hygiene activities

How do personal hygiene and talking to your child about their changing body relate? If your child can understand why they are suddenly being asked to wear deodorant or cleanse their face, they are more likely to do them. This grounds the activity and helps it to make sense. We are more likely to do something that makes sense to us, versus just being told to do it. Make sure that as you describe these things you do so in a fun, exciting way. Explain that these changes are perfectly normal and wonderful, and a sign that they are growing into a beautiful woman or handsome young man.

Growing up is fun

Growing up—becoming older—is a motivator for all children, including our children with autism. Highlight to them how they are growing up and how proud you are of them, and help them feel proud to be a teenager or young adult. Let them know that with this new stage in life comes fun self-grooming activities, such as wearing deodorant and choosing how you want to wear your hair, even maybe wearing hair gel. That now they are a teenager or young adult they get to choose different fun things at the pharmacy and then they get to use them on a daily basis.

Make a special trip to the pharmacy with them to pick out their new products. Let them have control over what they choose—they will more likely use it if they feel that they have chosen it. Couple this trip with a celebratory event marking this milestone in their development. Maybe it will be a trip to their favorite restaurant or a family dinner at home in their honor.

Make it cool to be clean

This is a different twist on making friends with the activity. Make it cool to be clean. Stay away from talking about the negative aspects of being dirty, such as people making fun of you if you smell; instead emphasize the positive effects of being clean. Do this not in the form of a lecture but through different activities and weaving it subtly into everyday situations and conversations. When the conversation gets round to movie stars, athletes, football stars, and pop stars, talk about how handsome and clean they are. Take notice and pass a complimentary comment when other family members have just taken a bath, styled their hair nicely, or are all dressed up to go out.

Take the hippest person in your child's life—maybe it is a cousin or another family member, or a friend of their sibling. If you think this person would be open, ask them to model how clean they like to be. For instance, they could come round and talk about which deodorant they use, or what type of gel they use on their hair. It is important that it is a person that your child looks up to and identifies with being cool.

When your child is clean and doing the hygiene activities you want them to, comment on how nice they smell or cool and handsome they look.

Get your child interested in how they present themselves by gathering pictures of different people they might relate to or admire. If your child is into drawing cartoons or is an artist, gather pictures of different artists. If your child likes athletes, gather pictures of different athletes, musicians, and so forth. While you look at the pictures together, discuss how each person presents differently and ask your child how they would like to present themselves. You could do this with pictures of your family members, discussing the difference between how each person looks, what style of clothes they like to wear, whether they are messy or tidy, etc., again asking your child how they want to present themselves.

Model how much you enjoy being clean yourself

After you have taken a shower, share with your child how great the shower felt on your skin, and how nice it feels to be clean and wear clean clothes. Comment on how you like the way your skin smells after using the new smelling soaps.

For all you dads out there, share and model how you enjoy taking care of your beard.

Moms, share with your daughter how fun it is to find the perfect skin cream for your face and how good your face feels afterwards.

Model how you wear deodorant, making sure you smell good before you leave the house. Model all the steps you do to take care of your adult body that you previously might not have thought to share with your child. Now is the time!

SELF-HELP SKILLS ACTION CHECKLIST

- ❏ See all self-help skills as important and valuable for your child—not something just to get over and done with.
- ❏ Think the following thoughts:
  - ❏ They are a step toward independence for my child.
  - ❏ They will translate into me having more time.
  - ❏ They can help strengthen my relationship with my child.
  - ❏ They can help my child become more socially successful.
- ❏ Make your own self-grooming activities fun for you by doing the following:
  - ❏ Get in the moment.
  - ❏ Find one thing to enjoy about the activity.
  - ❏ Anticipate what you enjoy about the activity just before you do it again.
  - ❏ Slow down the activity and really savor the part you enjoy.
  - ❏ Praise yourself for doing a great job at the self-grooming activity.
  - ❏ Share what you enjoyed about the activity to a family member or friend.
- ❏ Make it fun for your child by using your child's motivations.

❑ Make your child's sensory experience easier by buying unscented hypoallergenic products and having warm, soft towels.

❑ Go into your bathroom and check out the sensory experience that your child may be having.

❑ Ask your child about their experience if they can talk.

❑ Take the fight out of the equation—never force—and use the Control Protocol at all times.

❑ Help your child make friends with the activity. Doing this may let them explore the item without the threat of it being used on them. Play fun, motivating games with the item to help your child relax and make friends with the object.

❑ Ask your child to interact with the item once they have made friends with it.

Toothbrushing action checklist

❑ Give control—do not force.

❑ Be gentle when brushing your child's teeth.

❑ Model loving brushing your own teeth.

❑ Use the two-part games to help your child make friends and have fun with the toothbrush.

❑ Persist asking your child to brush their teeth in a fun and relaxed way each night and morning. Always respect any indication of "No."

Getting dressed action checklist

❑ Allow plenty of time.

❑ Get them dressed first in the morning, before breakfast, playing, and any electronics.

❑ Put your child's clothes out the night before.

❏ Ask your child to get dressed.

❏ Break it down: start with little steps and build up to bigger ones.

❏ Be playful and fun as you ask and get them dressed.

❏ Model getting dressed yourself.

❏ Bring your clothes into your child's room so you can get dressed together.

❏ Celebrate! Celebrate! Celebrate!

Bathtime action checklist

❏ Choose a bathtime that works for you.

❏ Decide beforehand that you are going to have fun and be relaxed at bathtime.

❏ Give your child prior warning that bathtime will be in 30 minutes.

❏ Don't start an activity that your child has a hard time transitioning away from just before bathtime.

❏ Let them bring their ism/stim toy into the bath with them.

❏ Make it fun! Try some of the fun bathtime ideas.

Hair washing action checklist

❏ Let go of any "need" you may have for your child to wash their hair.

❏ Give control.

❏ Get creative with different ways of presenting washing their hair. Try some of the suggestions found earlier in the chapter.

❏ Desensitize their head.

Hair cutting action checklist

- ☐ Help them make friends with the process. Try some of the games found earlier in the chapter.

- ☐ Let go of any need for your child to have a certain haircut.

- ☐ Give control; respect any indication they give you that they do not want their hair cut.

- ☐ Start with just one snip when your child is ready to begin getting their hair cut. Celebrate, and then next time do two snips, and so forth.

Nail cutting checklist

- ☐ Give control to your child by following the Control Protocol when you attempt to cut their nails.

- ☐ Help your child make friends with the activity by trying some of the games outlined in that section.

- ☐ Try cutting your child's nail during or after bath time.

Adolescent hygiene action checklist

- ☐ Talk to your child about the different ways their bodies are changing. Do this with an open, excited attitude.

- ☐ Explain the whys behind the new hygiene activities they now get to do.

- ☐ Make a special trip to the pharmacy so that they get to pick out their new products.

- ☐ Make it cool to be clean.

- ☐ Model how you love doing all these new hygiene activities.

Chapter 12

INTRODUCING NEW FOODS

Is your child a picky eater? Do they eat only three different food items, or limit themselves to just one? Maybe it's a certain brand of chocolate chip cookie, grilled cheese sandwich, or chicken nuggets only from McDonald's. Maybe your child's diet is a little more varied but does not consist of a single vegetable or fresh fruit. Does your child have chronic diarrhea or constipation, or maybe both? If you want to find a way to introduce new foods into your child's diet then this is the chapter for you. These techniques have helped countless parents help their children eat not only a varied diet, but also a healthy one.

Just last week I was consulting with a family whose child previously ate only white bread, cheese sticks, and pizza. They implemented all the suggestions in this chapter. Now he eats fish, chicken, beef, chickpeas, rice, quinoa, broccoli, green beans, tomatoes, kale, and onions, and loves his fresh "green juice" drink with a dash of lemon juice. The family have seen an increase in his ability to focus and interact. His verbal communication has improved and he is tantruming less. A good healthy diet can make a tremendous difference to your child's autism.

CONSIDER FOOD SENSITIVITIES

During my 25 years of working with children on the spectrum I have seen a great increase in children with digestive challenges. It is now commonplace for me to work with a child who has an extended stomach, dark circles under their eyes, or chronic constipation or diarrhea. Any one of these could be a symptom of a digestive challenge, and a sign that your child has food allergies/sensitivities. Your child restricting their diet to a few items can also be a sign of food allergies/sensitivities.

A study indicated that children on the autism spectrum are four times more likely to experience GI complaints compared with their peers. They are also three times more likely to experience constipation and diarrhea and complain twice as much about abdominal pain (McElhanon *et al.* 2014).

If your child is a picky eater, or has constipation, diarrhea, and/or an extended/bloated stomach, it is likely that the foods that they are eating are part of the challenge. It will be important to look into not only introducing new foods but also eliminating certain food types. The most common food types that our children have sensitivities to are gluten, casein, and sugar.

Gluten and casein

Gluten and casein are complex proteins found respectively in wheat and dairy products. There is much literature available online and in numerous books detailing the effect these two proteins have on children with autism. Putting it simply, some children with autism have a permeable gut, which means that there are tiny holes in the lining of their intestines. The proteins from gluten and casein enter our children's blood stream through these holes. These proteins then cross the blood–brain barrier and create morphine-like states in our children. So for our children these foods are like drugs. No wonder our children have a hard time focusing and interacting with others!

Some of you may be thinking, "Wow! All my child eats is wheat and dairy!" This is not uncommon. If your child has sensitivities to wheat and dairy, they are most likely addicted to these, and are actually craving them like you would any addictive drug. Take heart for once you remove these food items from your child's diet the cravings will disperse and they will start to eat other foods! This chapter will guide you through how to do this.

Sugar

Sugar is thought to be extremely addictive, and is often a major ingredient in processed foods. In the early 1800s, the average American consumed about 12 pounds of sugar per year. According to US Department of Agriculture (USDA) statistics, the average consumption of sugar, including corn sweeteners such as high fructose corn syrup, increased to more than 150 pounds per person by the year 2000 (USDA 2003). This perhaps also represents an increase in highly processed foods. How does this affect your child?

If our children are eating a lot of sugar this can prevent them from eating more healthy foods. If I am craving sugar I will look for the sugary food and push aside the vegetable or meat. Decreasing your child's intake of sugar will help them open up more easily to the new foods you are offering them.

Our children have digestive challenges; if your child has chronic diarrhea or constipation it is a sign that something is not quite right with their digestion. Sugar has also been proven to aid an overgrowth of a particular genus of fungus named Candida. This can cause our children to be physically uncomfortable and to have stomachaches. When we have a stomachache it is hard for us to learn new things and interact with others. This is no different for our children. Candida is often associated with dysbiosis and an excessive intake of sugar or refined carbohydrates. Candida overgrowth can cause many common symptoms including impaired memory and concentration (Truss 1981, 1984).

Sugar can also create energy highs and lows in our children's bodies. When working with children who have just eaten sugar, I will usually see an immediate surge in energy; the children become considerably less able to focus and very hyperactive, only to have what we call a "sugar crash" afterwards, and then become very lethargic. Again, this is not helping our children focus, interact, and learn new things—which is another excellent reason to reduce your child's sugar intake.

Sugars can be found in most if not all processed foods, including vegetable and meat products. Juices and processed drinks, including soya and rice milk, can have a high sugar content. I recommend that you look at the labels on your child's food to check for its sugar content. Below is a list of all the different words there are for sugar— some you will recognize, some you may not:

- Dextrose
- fructose
- galactose
- glucose

- lactose
- levulose
- maltose
- saccharose

- sucrose
- xylose
- mannitol
- sorbitol
- xylitol
- beet sugar
- brown sugar
- cane sugar
- confectionery sugar
- corn sugar
- corn sweetener
- corn syrup
- dehydrated cane juice
- dextrin
- fruit juice concentrate
- granulated sugar
- high fructose corn syrup
- honey
- invert sugar
- isomalt
- malt syrup
- maltodextrin
- maple sugar
- maple syrup
- molasses
- raw sugar
- rice syrup
- sorghum
- treacle
- turbinado sugar.

Reduce your child's sugar intake slowly

If you find that your child's sugar intake is particularly high, reduce it slowly. Just like any other substance, our body is addicted to it—it will be too hard on your child's body to go cold turkey. If your child drinks a lot of juice or soda and eats cookies and chocolate, eliminate one at a time. For instance, in the first week eliminate cookies from her diet; the second week keep the cookies out of her diet and remove all sodas; and then keep adding one item week by week until you have eliminated all of them.

Go to an autism doctor

In order to know if your child has sensitivities to gluten or casein, or to any other food types, it will be useful for you to consult with an autism doctor—one who believes that diet plays an important role in your child's autism and one who knows what test to use to identify any food sensitivities your child may have. One way to find out information about who would be a good autism doctor for you to consult with would be to use the numerous message boards online and ask other parents who they would recommend and why.

AUTISM DIETS

If you find that your child has sensitivities to certain foods, then eliminating the offending foods from their diet will not only help them with their health challenges but will help them open up to the new foods you want them to eat. There is much information about certain autism diets on the web and many books written on the subject.

Below are four of the most cutting-edge autism dietary interventions for autism. Each diet is designed to help your child with different health issues. I am not suggesting that you put your child on one of these diets, just that you research and educate yourself and come to your own conclusion. That way you can make the most informed decision for your child. The interventions are the:

- gluten-free, casein-free diet (GFCF)

- specific carbohydrate diet (SCD)

- GAPS diet

- body ecology diet.

Here is a great website that talks in depth about these and other autism diets for your child: http://nourishinghope.com.

Get prepared to start a new diet

If you do decide to eliminate certain foods from your child's diet the following steps will help you be successful.

1. **Start only when you are ready.** Changing your child's diet can be a big step, one that will positively affect your whole family. Some of you will learn about foods that you may not have heard about before. You know you are ready to begin when you have no doubts. It is important to be certain that the diet you are putting your child on will be helpful and

healthful for her. Researching in depth the diet and chatting with parents online who have put their children on the diet will help you be the most educated in its usefulness for your child. Our children are expert on picking up on our doubts. If they sense that we do not really mean that they will not be eating their usual food, they will wait us out by not eating. If we have doubts, we will let these doubts talk us into giving our children the foods they crave. We tell ourselves that it is better that they eat something than nothing at all. Feeding our children is at the very center of parenting. Giving our children the foods that they love can be an expression of our caring and love. I completely understand that it can be difficult not giving our children the food that we know they will eat when they are refusing to eat anything else. What we forget is that these foods are harming our children and are contributing to their autism. They do not nourish them. We also fear that they will never eat again. Our children may give us their best effort to convincing us of this. However, I have never experienced a child who has never eaten again because they were put on one of the above diets. I have however encountered many parents who will give their children the foods that they are craving.

I worked with a mom of a four-year-old boy called John. He would only eat cheese, fish crackers, and chicken nuggets, and was extremely constipated. She decided to put her child on a gluten-free and casein-free diet but was very scared and concerned about her child not eating. She took the plunge and began. Three days later her child had still not eaten anything and was lying on the floor listless, looking very sorry for himself. Concerned that she would give in to her fears and give him the food she knew he would eat, she called me for support. We talked about her fears that John would never eat again, and that she should as his mother give him any food he wanted. By the end of the call she had reaffirmed her commitment to helping him by not giving him foods that were harmful for him even though he wanted them. She also held the belief that he would not starve himself forever. She emailed me the next day saying that he ate his first slice of gluten-free toast that morning for breakfast. Her attitude and commitment made a difference. By the end of the first week on a gluten-free and casein-free diet John tried ten new foods, including cucumbers, lettuce, and green beans, and his eye contact had greatly improved. Now those are food types that really are nourishing for John's body.

We want to communicate with our attitude that we really are not giving them the old food. Our children need to sense that we really mean business and that things have changed. This will help them move on and accept the new food situation.

2. **Educate yourself.** You now know what foods you want your child not to eat. Now educate yourself on the foods that your child can eat and also the different meals and recipes you can create and cook for your child. Any Internet search will generate lots of great gluten- and casein-free recipes you can try with your child.

    The DVD *Let's Go Shopping: Special Foods for Special Needs ADHD, PDD-NOS, Autism, Celiac Disease & Down Syndrome* will guide you through the shelves of a health food store. The mom who created this DVD has a son with autism, and her son actually asks for his "green algae drink."

3. **Get your kitchen ready.** Get all the food you do not want your child to eat out of the house. If these foods are in your house, your child will find them and eat them. I have heard numerous stories of children finding foods that have been hidden in attics and garages. If these foods are not in your house, it will also be easier for you not to give them to your child. This also helps to eliminate any control battles that may arise once your child finds the food.

    What about the other members of your household—your other children and your partner? To make this transition the most effective for your child with autism, make it family-wide. Sugar is not healthy for your other children or spouse. I know of two great parents who went on the same diet they put their daughter on and they both lost 25 pounds. They report feeling healthier, happier, and more able to focus. This is good news for the whole family. That does not mean that everyone has to go on a total diet—just when they are in the house. When your other children are at school or elsewhere they can eat what they want. This will also save you from cooking many different meals.

4. **Explain to your child why you are changing their diet.** Let them know the reasons behind these new foods. If your child has food intolerances, they will have had some internal discomfort. If they are constipated or have diarrhea, this will also be the case. Let them know that the new foods will help them feel more comfortable. It is ok if they do not appear to be listening, trust that they are (see Chapter 5.) Let them know that you are on their side and are doing this to help them. My godchild has had many food allergies at different stages in her life that have caused her physical pain, as well as physical consequences such as diarrhea. Knowing this, she has been self-motivated to keep away from these foods and listen to her parents' guidance. I see this quality in many children with autism.

Explain all the same reasons to your other children. Let them know that their participation in eating the new diet at home will greatly help their siblings—that this can be their contribution to the wellbeing of their brother or sister. Let them also know the great benefits to their health of eating this diet. They will become fitter, smarter, and live longer than their peers! If you are to get family-wide participation they will need all the information.

AVOID A GLUTEN- AND CASEIN-FREE JUNK FOOD DIET

This is going to be key. Once you have taken away the foods that your child is allergic to, there will be other snack foods and numerous gluten- and casein-free products on the market that may have very high sugar levels. I would encourage you to limit the amount of gluten-free products, such as pancakes, cookies, waffle mixes, cup cakes, pretzels, bread rolls, and chicken nuggets, to a minimum. These products are often highly processed and can be filled with sugar that is addictive for our children—the same for snacks such as popcorn, potato chips, and the like. I have worked with families whose children previously only ate three foods, all of which they were allergic to; once they were successfully eliminated from their diet, they were replaced with three other foods, which were pancakes, chicken nuggets, and potato chips—all gluten-free and casein-free but still not a varied or healthy diet.

My suggestion to you would be to keep to real foods instead of packaged products. If you provide meats, grains, and vegetables for your child, it is more likely that they will eat a healthy and varied diet once the allergies are removed from their diet.

HOW TO INTRODUCE NEW FOODS
Give control

Eating is something that we cannot force our children to do. It is within their control only. Have you ever had someone thrust a fork with a piece of food on it close to your face with the insistence that you taste it? Usually our first reaction is to push it away, and examine what it is before we let it inside our bodies. Our initial response is no. Asking our child to eat is a big request. We are more likely to be successful if we are easy and relaxed when presenting food, by asking our children to eat in a non-pushy, non-pressure way.

That means not forcing our children to eat, or suddenly popping something in their mouths. Above all, respect any indication of "No, I do not want to eat this." This might be your child turning their head away, pressing their lips together, pushing the food away, or simply just saying, "No." Remember, giving control actually helps our children want to do what we are asking them to do.

Love the new food yourself

There is simply something so appealing about another person really enjoying eating their meal. I have spent many an evening at a restaurant wishing I had ordered the same dish as my friend just based on their exclamations of delight. It is time to make your peace with vegetables, quinoa, millet, rice, and all the new foods you will be offering to your child and learn to love eating them. If you think they are disgusting, why should your child eat them?

Demonstrate this love by eating the new foods in front of your child. Do this with relish as if you were eating your most favorite dish. Make big "I love this food" facial expressions. Lick your lips and tell them how delicious it is. We want to sell this food. We want to be the best advertisement possible.

Be easy and super non-invasive

This means not pouncing on your child and offering food really close to their face. If your child comes over to a plate of food, do not immediately ask them to eat it or pick up the food from the plate and offer it to them. Be silent and give them time to investigate it. Maybe smile at them as a silent way of encouraging them to investigate the food. If you talk and offer straight away, your child may walk away from your request. It is my experience that when I give a child time, they will try the food themselves without my insistence. You may find that your child comes over, looks at it, and walks away; again, trust them—it may take them four or five times of looking at the food before they decide to take a bite. If we get in the way of this process, they may not try at all.

Another way is to put a piece of food on a fork and offer it to your child from a few feet away. Then let them come to the fork and decide for themselves whether they are going to just look at it, touch it, put it up to their lips, or eat it. All of these actions are steps in the eating process. All exciting! All worth celebrating!

Have food easily available to your child

This is so crucial. Let's not just have food available at mealtimes, let's have food readily available. Place bowls of the new food around the house. This will help your child get used to the new look and smells. The more familiar your child is with the food, the more likely they will investigate it. Having food readily available may also tempt them when they are really hungry. I would encourage you to make this available food plentiful. Put at least two bowls in the room your child is in. The bowls can contain foods such as quinoa, rice (if this is permissible on the diet you have chosen), cut-up cucumbers, nuts, cooked vegetables, or a little cut-up chicken.

Remember, love the new food yourself! When you are with your child, stop every now and then and munch on some of the food. If your child has been very controlling around trying new foods, do not attempt to offer the food to them—just model how delicious it is.

If your child is hungry, the combination of available food, you eating it in a tempting way, and having control can be very powerful in encouraging your child to eat the new food.

Get creative

There are so many different ways to cook and present each food. You never know which way your child will like. For instance, I do not like cooked carrots but I love raw carrots, and there are many more ways to be creative with carrots:

- raw, cut up in circles

- grated

- diced in small squares

- cut up in shapes to create pictures like a face or a space rocket

- cooked whole

- baked

- steamed

- mashed with a little salt and pepper

- sautéd with a little garlic and oil

- carrot soup.

For a child who has challenges with textures, try to offer foods that only have one texture. For example, a tomato has three textures: the skin, the pips, and the flesh. If you offer an apple or other fruits, peel it and take out the pips. The same goes for vegetables. With meats, try also to make it one texture, cutting away the fats and making sure it is one color. This may help your child eat the food presented.

There are many different ways to encourage your child to eat the same food. Don't give up! If your child does not eat it one way, try another.

Consider ways to make the grain or meat or vegetable tastier. Sautéing the food adds flavor; herbs and different seasoning can make the food more appealing to your child. Just because it is healthy does not mean that it has to be tasteless.

Experiment

Experiment with how many foods you put on your child's plate at mealtimes. Some children will only eat when there is one food type on a plate. If there are more than one, they refuse to eat. If your child has challenges with textures, this will probably be the case.

Print out pictures of things that your child really likes and put them on the plate next to the food. This could encourage your children to come over and start investigating the food.

Let them get up from the table and run in between bites. Often our children have to move; if we put them in a situation where we do not allow them to move, they may reject the food, however hungry, just so they can leave the table and move. If you let them get up and run, you may just find that they come back in a few moments for another bite. Moving can aid in digestion; for some of our children who are having digestion issues, they are probably taking care of themselves in the most amazing way.

You might be thinking: "But then how will she ever learn to sit and eat at the table?" Let's work on one thing at a time. Let's first help them eat a healthier diet; once we have done that, we can work on helping them to sit and eat at the table.

Sometimes sitting down beside your child while they are isming/stimming, and letting them know that they can carry on with what they are doing and that you are just going to help them eat, works wonders. After you have explained what you are going to do, gently put the spoon or fork up to their mouths and wait for them to open their mouths. You can also gently say, "Open your mouth so I can help you eat this yummy food." If your child does this, then proceed and feed them this way; if they do not, or push you away, give control and do not force-feed them in any way.

Examine your family mealtime from a sensory perspective. If you have a big family, chances are that it is loud and over-stimulating for your child with autism. If this is the case, consider the idea that your child is not ready to thrive during family meals. It may be easier for your child to concentrate on eating their meal if they are in a non-distracting environment. I would suggest that you give your child their meal before the rest of the family—in the kitchen with just you or your partner, or in another room in the house. Close the door of the kitchen or room so that she cannot wander all around the house. In this smaller and quieter environment you will be more able to concentrate on helping her eat.

Bring the new food into playtime

Get a little loose with what you can do with food. The more your child touches and interacts with the food, the more comfortable they will become with the idea of eating it. Below are some ideas for you to try. Remember to modify them to suit your child's motivations.

- If your child likes trains, you could pretend the vegetables are passengers waiting to board the train.

- You could also pretend that the vegetables are cargo being dropped of at different stores.

- You could attach a balloon to paper food parcels, making hot air balloons that land on your child's plate.

- If your child likes to draw, cook some carrots and beets and use them as vegetable paints or crayons.

- Juggle with grapes or berries or apples.

- Have your child's favorite characters dive into a bowl of quinoa to save an animal from drowning.

- Set up a treasure hunt for your child, where the treasure is a small item that is buried in a bowl of new food.

- Have a real-food picnic with all the soft animals in the room.

As an example of how you could modify these examples to suit your child's motivations, think about how you could include food with the toys that they like. For example, if they like figurines, you could make a little snack for each figurine. Give each snack to your child to offer to their figurine. If your child likes balls you could pretend that a grape or an apple is a ball and roll it to each other or play catch.

It's ok if things get a little messy. The important thing is that we are having fun with the food—that we are presenting it to our child in an easy, fun, and super-relaxed way. Taking the pressure away from you and your child will allow any tension that may have grown around eating to fade away. That's when the eating can begin.

TROUBLESHOOTING

? *My child will sometimes refuse to eat even the food she likes.*

I have worked with many children who once they have gone without food for too long will reject all offers. Sometimes our children are unable to tell us that they are hungry, or maybe do not recognize the feeling of hunger inside themselves. This can affect their blood sugar levels and they can begin to get very lethargic, or they can shut down. One way to help a child eat under these circumstances is to spoon food into their mouths while they are involved in another activity. They may be stimming/isming by flipping pages in a book, drawing, or lining up letters. While they are doing this, quietly sit beside them and without interrupting their activity feed them. Of course, we would still give them control and look for permission. After you have explained what you are going to do, gently put the spoon or fork up to their mouth and wait for them to open their mouth. You can also gently say, "Open your mouth so I can help you eat this yummy food." If your child does this, then proceed and feed them this way; if they do not, or push you away, give control and do not force-feed them in any way. Most times I find that a child will allow the food if they can concentrate on something else. This helps to get food into the system and bring balance to their blood sugar.

To avoid getting in this situation I would suggest that you offer your child food every two hours. This way your child will not get into the situation of becoming too hungry to eat.

? *My child will only eat pureed food. How do I get her to eat solid food?*

This could be a combination of a sensory challenge and the autistic challenge of dealing with change. The key here would be to slowly increase the consistency of the food toward solid food. Going straight from pureed food to solid or lumpy food is too big a jump. Increase the thickness first without making it lumpy. If your child allows this, then slowly make it lumpy and work from there.

If your child only eats pureed food and has shown no ability to chew, it may be because of low muscle tone in the mouth. If this is the case, there are many exercises that you can do with your child to increase the muscle tone of her mouth. The idea is to get the mouth active and build up stamina in the muscles—that way your child will be able to sustain the activity of chewing. Some ideas:

- Have fun blowing musical instruments. The lip whistle is a great toy as it makes a noise if you blow in or out. You can also have fun with the penny whistle, kazoo, and harmonica.

- Encourage your child to drink through a straw.

- Have a race to see who can blow a tissue paper ball through a straw into a goal the quickest.

- Make funny faces moving your mouth in the mirror. Growl like a lion or chirp like a bird.

- Before you start any of the above games, massage your child's mouth and jaw. This will help wake the area up and bring your child's attention to their mouth.

INTRODUCING NEW FOODS ACTION CHECKLIST

- ❏ Check to see if your child has food sensitivities with an autism doctor.

- ❏ Consider eliminating gluten, casein, and sugar from your child's diet.

- ❏ Research the different autism diets:
    - ❏ Consider the gluten-free, casein-free diet.
    - ❏ Consider the specific carbohydrate diet.
    - ❏ Consider the GAPS diet.
    - ❏ Consider the body ecology diet.

- ❏ Get prepared:
    - ❏ Believe 100 percent in the diet you choose.
    - ❏ Educate yourself on all the foods your child can eat.
    - ❏ Get your kitchen ready by getting rid of any food your child cannot eat.

- ❏ Explain to your child with autism her new diet and why it is going to be so great for her.

- ❏ Explain this new diet to the whole family and the benefits for them.

- ❏ Keep it to mostly "real" food, by avoiding packaged foods as much as possible.

- ❏ Give control when introducing new foods.

- ❏ Love the new foods! Model eating them and how yummy they are.

- ❏ Be super-easy and non-invasive when offering the new food.

- ❏ Have the new food easily available to your child.

- ❏ Get creative with how you present and cook the food.

- ❏ Experiment with different ways of giving your child the food.

- ❏ Bring food into playtime.

RECOMMENDED READING AND VIEWING

Autism Breakthrough: The Groundbreaking Method That Has Helped Families All Over the World by Raun K. Kaufman

Autism Micro Tutorials: Bite-sized Son-Rise Program Techniques by the Autism Treatment Center of America (DVD)

Games4Socialization: Using the Son-Rise Program Developmental Model by the Autism Treatment Center of America (DVD)

Breakthrough Strategies for Autism Spectrum Disorders by Raun K. Kaufman (DVD)

Inspiring Journeys of Son-Rise Program Families (Free DVD)

Autism Solutions (Free DVD)

Son-Rise: A Miracle of Love (NBC-TV movie; available on amazon.com)

Three books by Barry Neil Kaufman: *Son-Rise: The Miracle Continues, A Miracle to Believe In,* and *Happiness Is a Choice*

The Autism Treatment Center YouTube channel has hundreds of videos filled with creative ideas and games to help your child on the autism spectrum. You can view them at www.youtube.com/user/autismtreatment

REFERENCES

Cespedes, E.M., Gillman, M.W., Kleinman, K., Rifas-Shiman, S.L., Redline, S., and Taveras, E.M. (2014) "Television viewing, bedroom television and sleep duration from infancy and mid childhood." *Pediatrics* [Epub ahead of print].

Dunbar, R.I.M., Baron, R., Frangou, A., Pearce, E. *et al.* (2012) "Social laughter is correlated with an elevated pain threshold." *Proceedings of the Royal Society B 279*, 1731, 1161–1167. doi:10.1098/rspb.2011.1373.

The Early Childhood Initiative Foundation, *Special Needs*. Available at www.teachmorelovemore.org/SpecialNeedsDetails.asp?id=3, accessed on 26 November 2014.

Fleischmann, A. (2012) *Carly's Voice: Breaking Through Autism*. New York, NY: Touchstone.

Higashida, N. (2013) *The Reason I Jump: One Boy's Voice from the Silence of Autism*. London: Hodder & Stoughton.

Kaufman, R.K. (2014) *Autism Breakthrough: The Groundbreaking Method That Has Helped Families All Over the World*. New York, NY: St. Martin's Press.

McElhanon, B.O., McCracken, C., Karpen, S., and Sharp, W.G. (2014) "Gastrointestinal symptoms in autism spectrum disorder: A meta-analysis." *Pediatrics 133*, 5, 872.

Rosenthal, R. and Babad, E.Y. (1985) "Pygmalion in the gymnasium." *Educational Leadership 41*, 1, 36–39.

Rosenthal, R. and Jacobson, L. (1968) *Pygmalion in the Classroom: Teacher Expectations and Pupils' Intellectual Development*. New York, NY: Holt, Rinehart and Winston.

Sleep for Kids (ND) *Information About Children's Sleep for Parents and Teacher*. Available at www.sleepforkids.org/html/sheet.html, accessed on 26 November 2014.

Thompson, D.A. and Christakis, D.A. (2005) "The association between television viewing and irregular sleep schedules among children less than 3 years old." *Pediatrics 116*, 4, 851–856.

Truss, C.O. (1981) "The role of Candida albicans in human illness." *Journal of Orthomolecular Psychiatry 10*, 4, 228–238.

Truss, C.O. (1984) "Metabolic abnormalities in patients with chronic candidiasis: The acetaldehyde hypothesis." *Journal of Orthomolecular Psychiatry 13*, 2, 66–93.

United States Department of Agriculture (USDA) (2003) "Profiling Food Consumption in America." In *Agriculture Factbook 2001–2002* (pp.12–21). Washington, DC: USDA.

van der Helm, E., Gujar, N., and Walker, M.P. (2010) "Sleep deprivation impairs the accurate recognition of human emotions." *Sleep 33*, 3, 335–342.